ONE
YELLOW
DOOR

First published in 2015 by
Darton, Longman and Todd Ltd
1 Spencer Court
140–142 Wandsworth High Street
London SW18 4JJ

ISBN 978–0–232–53205–0

A catalogue record for this book is available from the British Library.

Phototypeset by Kerrypress Ltd
Printed and bound by Bell & Bain, Glasgow.

ONE YELLOW DOOR

*A memoir of love and loss,
faith and infidelity*

Rebecca de Saintonge

DARTON · LONGMAN + TODD

David Chaput de Saintonge
In memoriam

CONTENTS

Acknowledgements

I cannot even begin to express my thanks to the following people: Professor Praveen Anand, Professor Tina Beattie, Dave Beattie, Dea Birkett, Dr Richard Croft, Joan Deitch, Hester Green, Bob and Georgia Hayes, Dr Michael Maltby, Revd Tony Rutherford, Becky Swift, Patsy Trench, my publisher David Moloney, and finally to my husband Robin Hare, who makes me laugh in ways only he and Squeaker know about, and whose love and generous spirit have given me so much encouragement.

Prologue

The poet, said Thomas Merton, enters into himself that he may create. The contemplative enters into God to be created.

What a terrifying concept, to willingly allow yourself to be created, re-created, by the God who is silent in the face of disintegration. Were you re-created, Jack, when you were being taken apart, piece by piece? First your feet, then your legs, then your bladder, then your heart, then your power to write, then your power to read, then your power to speak, then your powers to reason. When you were left only with an all-pervading sense of helplessness and mental anguish, was this God creating you, re-creating you?

And if so, for what? And am I now, now that it is over and your body has been burnt to a fistful of dust, am I too to submit my will to this 'creating' God?

I think not.

PART ONE

Different Planets

A strange courtship

I loved his big, loose hands. I loved the way they moved across the paper when he was drawing. His long johns were cherry red. I bought them for him as a wedding present to match the fingerless gloves I knitted so he could paint outdoors in winter. The days seemed to dance by.

It's funny, but when I think of Jack now, I always think of colours. You know that blue of a high winter sky? Not vivid, but clear. Those were his eyes. His hair was thick and prematurely white, and his voice, his voice was moss green, the gentle, melting voice of a Welsh tenor. Only one grandparent was Welsh, as it happens, but he had inherited that extraordinary timbre, so unselfconsciously sensual. His power as an orator, I'm sure, was as much due to the music in his voice as to the words that he spoke. Though his words could set you free. No doubt about that. One man told me that Jack had changed his life forever.

We came from different planets. My father was a diplomat, his a jobbing bricklayer. My mother choreographed mimes and let the washing go mouldy in the clothes-basket; his baked wonderful rice puddings and sent him out for jellied eels. There was something solid about his working-class roots that gave him a grounded commonsense, while my parents, magic though they were, had not one ounce of emotional intelligence between them. At first I thought him a bit slow on the uptake, he never seemed to understand what I was going on about. Then I realised it was just that Jack was sane.

He had an almost slap-happy *joie de vivre* that set you free. When he first discovered that my fridge door only shut if you put a chair in front of it, he hauled me into his battered old car – which was blue except for the rear passenger door which was yellow (a junk yard replacement after a prang) – and drove down to the industrial estate, pointed at the first fridge he saw and said, 'We'll have that one'. No agonising evenings poring over *Which?* magazine like my first husband. It was just a fridge, for heaven's sake! Buy the bloody thing.

But in the same way that you can't describe a colour without reducing it to something less than it is, so you can't describe the complex, loving, innocent, passionate man who, while still struggling to get over the early death of his wife, walked into my own very broken life and gathered me up into this great bundle of laughter and energy and dedication. He was 51, twenty years my senior, but I still had to run to catch up with him.

I remember so well the first moment I did.

It was one of those rare summer days when the heat hangs breathless. I was leaning on the gate, an old jumper tied round my waist, gazing at the cornfield. It was violent with poppies. It reminded me of the first time I'd been kissed in a cornfield. I was thirteen, all bum and brassiere and his name was Larry. His breath smelled a bit, but it was still quite interesting.

On this particular day, because Jack had a way of bending slightly and looking directly into your eyes, I had taken great care with my mascara, making sure every lash on the lower lids was carefully delineated. I used the old-fashioned block and spit mascara that Max Factor used to sell. If you were careful, you could make it look as though you didn't have any make-up on at all.

Jack stood to one side, one foot tucked behind the other. He was clearly trying to look nonchalant, but there was a tension in his body, his eyes glancing first at me, then back at the road. We'd never been alone before, and I'd only ever seen him in his clerical shirt, and never with his sleeves rolled up. The sun glinted on the hairs of his arm and the sight of them was suddenly alarmingly intimate.

When we were surrounded by people, at meetings or social gatherings, we were forever sparking off one another, darting in and out of each other's conversations, but now we seemed paralysed by an awkward silence. Now that Jack was my boss I had tried to persuade myself that it was perfectly normal for us to take time out together, just in a relaxed, natural sort of way. The trouble was it didn't feel relaxed, or natural.

I twittered foolishly in the silences, wishing I'd shut up, but unable to.

'There's a pub up the road,' he said at last.

Thank God for that. The thought of a drink was clearly a relief to us both and we bumped up the road together, apologising each time our bodies touched, trying to keep a distance between us. Not keeping a distance between us.

A waitress came and smacked our fish and chips down on the little round table, the plates juggling for room with the beer mats and the packets of brown sauce and tomato ketchup. Jack unrolled his knife and fork from the paper napkin and paused, and for an awful moment I wondered if he was going to say grace. Then looking up, he met my rather hesitant glance.

'We can't marry, you know. Clergy are not allowed to marry divorced women.'

He looked stunned. The words had seemed to come, unbidden, from some deep, unexplored place. Jack had never given the slightest impression that he felt anything particular for me. It's true he flirted a lot, but with everyone, and with a sort of innocent largesse. Almost anyone passing could have come under his spell. Certainly no words of tenderness had ever passed between us. It was almost as if he hadn't known, until the words were spoken, that he felt anything at all, and the revelation shocked him.

The pupils of his eyes were very dark. I seemed to see only his eyes. There was no world around them. I knew then that he had recognised me at last. It was both wonderful, and in the circumstances, terrible. But for me it was not so much a surprise, as a relief. The truth is, I had recognised him a long time before.

It was to be a strange courtship. Shocked by our shared attraction we went to see the bishop. Me because I could not believe such a strong sense of connection could be wrong, and Jack because he could not believe it could be right. He was an Anglican priest, after all, and his vocation took precedence over everything else. The only possible way forward was if, despite all indications to the contrary, the bishop – under whose authority Jack was placed – gave us permission to meet.

To Jack's astonishment he did. 'The church is sometimes wrong you know,' he smiled, 'and I see God in your relationship. Be circumspect, and come and see me again.'

Two years were to pass before our wedding day, but during that time, if ever an obstacle was raised in our path, I was filled with a deep sense that all would be well. I had submitted myself to the authority of the church and received its blessings, and by the end of that two years the church had changed its laws, and our marriage could go ahead.

My dear Jack – before I met you my life seemed like a train pulling a trail of empty carriages, and then there you were, and suddenly most of them were full – with people and noise and laughter, with faith and vision and your extraordinary, electric vitality. You gathered me up, who had been a wife before, but not a wife, enfolded me in your understanding and joy of living, and for the next six years I followed you into a labyrinth of colours – to France, to America and finally, to Africa.

Before I met Jack I had worked for most of my life as a journalist, both in England and abroad, but shortly after we married I decided to try my luck writing books. I'd been approached by a publisher to be a ghost writer for a man called Pete Riley who had been a criminal minder in London. His job had been to watch the back of the Kray brothers – notorious London gangsters famed for their violence. Rather miraculously Pete had become a reformed character and I was to tell his story. This was my first stab at ghost writing – getting into the mind of another human being and trying to experience life through their eyes. Jack came into my study one day to find me lying on the floor with my hands clenched, palms upwards on my chest, my eyes screwed shut and my whole body jerking convulsively.

'Sweetheart, are you in pain?'

'No, I'm underneath a train.'

'What?'

'I'm escaping, and I'm hanging on to the underneath of a train. It's pulling out of the station. It's bloody uncomfortable.'

The second book got us both on our way. To Africa.

1982 Zimbabwe calls

During the war of independence in what was then Rhodesia, and is now Zimbabwe, Alec, the son of the white Prime Minister Ian Smith, had been working underground with Moral Rearmament as a sort of freelance diplomat. Alec loved his father but was fundamentally opposed to his politics and his attitude to black Rhodesians. Throughout the war he and his colleagues, black and white, worked with the guerrilla fighters, travelling deep into the bush, trying to build bridges of understanding between the warring factions. It was extremely dangerous work, especially for the son of the Prime Minister whom the guerrillas were trying to depose, but it says everything for Alec – and for the new regime – that when Independence was finally won, the deputy Prime Minister, Simon Muzenda, called Alec to his office and thanked him for his work. In those days Alec travelled everywhere in a yellow Volkswagen and Muzenda told him that throughout the war the guerrilla fighters were told to protect the man in the little yellow car.

Alec continued to keep in close contact with the new regime, as did his father who, unknown to the general population, had secret meetings with Robert Mugabe over many months to discuss the running of the country. The relationship between these two men – so violently and radically opposed – was, in those early days of Independence, unexpectedly creative, and came about through the vision, the courage and the humility of Alec and his friends. It's part of the Zimbabwean story very few people know.

So Alec Smith clearly had a story to tell, but a misspent youth heavily laced with LSD and a disinclination to put pen to paper made the writing of it somewhat problematical. I was asked by the publisher to help him out and so, eighteen months after Independence, Jack took a sabbatical month and accompanied me to the new Zimbabwe so that I could spend time gathering material for the book.

We talked to many Zimbabweans, black and white, who had been involved in the difficult processes of political transformation. I shall never forget walking into the office of Byron Hove, who had been a deputy Minister of Justice in the interim black government, and a friend of Alec's. He had a stunning collection of modern Zimbabwean sculptures. I had never seen Shona sculptures before. You have to touch them. The simplicity of line, the smoothness of stone, the deepness of the spirit they reveal, draw you like a magnet. I found myself walking round the room of this tall stranger stroking the stones while he talked about the artists who had fashioned them. We had less than an hour together, but it was one of those rare and unexpected meetings of minds that leaves you dazed by its intensity. At least I think it was minds … the little pat on my bottom as I made for the door made me wonder in retrospect if my approach to this interview had been, perhaps, just a little too tactile.

That meeting could not have been more different from the night we spent with Ian and Janet Smith on their farm in Bulawayo when Jack took a rather disorientated Janet Smith in his arms and waltzed her round the room to a tune on the radio.

That was typical of him. He was passionately opposed to the Smiths' politics. We were appalled, on visiting their farm, to find that the sheds in which the farming tackle was kept were smarter than the shacks that housed their workers. The men themselves, when they came to help in the kitchen, seemed to cower against the walls when you passed them, as if trying, somehow, not to exist.

But what Jack saw, as we sat in the sitting room after our simple supper, was a woman who appeared at that time to be as dispossessed as her servants. Beneath her immaculate exterior and well-honed social manners there was a lostness, as if she was suddenly alone in a fearful place and nothing was real any more. She seemed, almost, to be disintegrating, held together only by social etiquette. It was this fragility that Jack gathered up in an ungainly waltz when she expressed, with a smile, how when she was young she used to dance to the radio. Ungainly, I may say, because Jack didn't know how to waltz. He just whirled her round – much to her astonished delight.

For most of our visit we were hosted by Mike and Ann Macfarlane, a young Anglican minister and his wife who lived in a rather lovely district of Harare. Mike and Jack took to each other like father and son, so we were not entirely surprised when, six months after our return to England, with the book almost finished, the phone rang in our kitchen. It was Mike.

'Mike!' I shouted with delight, thinking somehow it necessary to raise my voice to cover the distance. 'You sound as if you're just down the road!'

'Well, funny you should say that.'

'Why?'

'We were just wondering if you'd come and join us for a couple of years.'

Zimbabwe is stunningly beautiful. The main streets of the capital, Harare, were originally designed to be wide enough to turn an ox cart, and all are lined with huge, exotic flowering trees – rows and rows of them; jacarandas which drop their lilac blooms in great swathes that carpet the pavements, fiery flamboyants and brilliant orange flame trees. Great clumps of poinsettia bloom casually by the roadside, six or seven feet tall, and the air is scented with the sweet almond perfume of the frangipani tree. Life in the townships, of course, is quite a different matter, as we were soon to discover.

We arrived two years after Independence. It was 1982 and the country at that time was a complex mixture of grief and hope as old Rhodesians struggled to become new Zimbabweans. There were terrible wounds on both sides of the racial divide – loved ones maimed and lost, lives and careers destroyed, and fear, anger and mistrust which somehow had to be transformed into a positive creative energy for the future.

Yet despite the pain, there was a tremendous sense of hope. In public, the Mugabe of those early years spoke with conviction about the need to forget the past and build a new future as partners. In private he was meeting with Ian Smith and other former ministers to work towards a stable future. There was no hint then of the horror he was to unleash two decades later.

Although Jack's sympathies always lay left of centre, he had a way of challenging the attitudes of others that didn't box them into a corner. Rather, he could communicate the vision and excitement of change and give people the confidence to believe they had the emotional energy to embrace it. Because of this – and, no doubt, because they enjoyed one another's company – Mike thought he would be an ideal colleague to work with through these delicate times. We were thrilled. We had both fallen in love with Zimbabwe and the thought of an adventure was intoxicating.

The first couple of years were fine. I did notice that Jack was relying on old ideas, but since they were new to the Zimbabwe congregation, it didn't seem to matter. And he still managed to sweep people along with his enthusiasm.

But I remember the day when what had been just a faint shadow of doubt in my mind, became a real concern.

African bougainvilleas don't do subtle. They shout their way up through the branches of trees in a clash of purple and vermillion, and then ramble all over the place, quite uncontrolled, like a bad hair day. This particular afternoon I was sitting in the garden gazing at them. I was taking a breather from a long morning and an interrupted night. Our single-storey house was one of the oldest in Harare, with pressed tin ceilings and a constant thread of ants from tap to sink. It was situated – gloriously, I thought – between heaven and hell, with the Baptist church on one side and the local brothel on the other. At three that morning there had been a tap tap on the bedroom window.

'Pleese Mees Becca, lend me forty dollaahs.'

'Bugger off, Charlotte.'

Tap, tap, tap.

'Pleese, pleese Mees Becca, lend me forty dollaahs. I need forty dollaahs.'

'BUGGER OFF, CHARLOTTE.'

I was quite fond of Charlotte. She was one of the regulars who consoled our gardener during the absence of his wife. What it took me a little while to realise was that he was doubling up on his income by turning the tiny shed next to his quarters into a mini-brothel. I simply couldn't understand why on most weekdays a different pair of men's shoes could be found neatly placed outside the shed, or why Aeroplane, that was his name, wanted to line the shed floor with cardboard. It took a quiet word from our Zimbabwean neighbours to alert us to his extra-curricular activities.

One of the many reasons why I wouldn't give Charlotte 'forty dollaahs' in the middle of the night was because she had, aided and abetted by Aeroplane, already nicked my long gold chain and wedding ring. Not that I blamed her in the least. Nor did Jack. It was our fault for leaving them around. We remembered what Martin Luther King had said, that it 'does violence to the human heart to live in poverty, amid plenty'. We had been thoughtless.

I was to remember this day particularly because it was the first indication that all was not well with Jack.

'I can't understand why I'm so stressed,' he'd said over lunch. 'Everything seems such an effort. Why do I get so anxious?'

He wasn't a man to navel gaze and just got on with life, but I noticed that he found it increasingly hard to be sociable. We stopped visiting friends. He began to lose his laughter, and his eyes, always so vital, were clouded. Five months later he was so anxious that he couldn't cross the road. I found him distressed and confused, unable to step off the pavement, looking fearfully at the passing traffic. 'I don't know what to do,' he said. 'Where am I supposed to go?'

Everyone diagnosed a breakdown, but Jack was not breakdown material, I knew that. Something very troubling was beginning to happen. We had been married nearly six years and for the first time I felt a growing disquiet

I rang my brother in England for his medical advice. Michael was a consultant physician at University College Hospital in London, but like most doctors, reluctant to advise his own family. This time it was different.

'Michael,' I said, 'what shall I do?' He didn't hesitate.

'Come home.'

Leaving an African country is not easy. It took six weeks to cut through all the red tape, and a lot of help from friends in high places. Jack was by this time barely functioning and left me to organise our departure. But the delay gave me time to visit the township where I'd worked and say goodbye to my friends. I'd set up an embroidery co-operative which by this time was providing a regular income to a handful of families who were now able to educate their children.

Monise, whom I loved, took me by the hand and led me through the mud streets to say a final farewell to the neighbours. We met four new babies, all called Rebecca. Monise was as thin as a twig. The joke was that she had no breasts, except on pay-day when she had one. This was because she always stuffed her money in the left side of her bra. She lived in a two-roomed concrete house with an outside latrine, but she could only live in one of the rooms because a relative had died in the other and she didn't have the money to pay for the necessary ceremony to spiritually cleanse it. In the one room she did inhabit – with her errant husband and two children – she had a handmade wooden bed, a stool, and a tiny gas stove for one pot. Today she was wearing blue plastic flip-flops. As we walked by the mealie patch near her house Monise glanced down at my red plimsoles. It was an old game we'd played before. Without saying anything we swapped shoes. Then we sat on the grass outside her hut, African-style, the ants biting our outstretched legs, with a teapot of Monise's special brew. As a treat she had bought some tea leaves and put them in the pot with hot water, boiled milk and two tablespoons of sugar.

When the co-operative met in her house the other women had refused to speak English. Time for me to learn Shona, they said. I struggled, and rarely understood a word, but it felt wonderfully comfortable to sit in that warm hubbub. I loved their harsh laughter and the way they slapped hands. They say

Westerners have problem-solving minds; Africans experience one another. 'Because you are, I am'. Certainly when I tried to run meetings with an agenda, setting out our objectives, our structures for quality control, our medium and long-term goals, they were a disaster. Once I'd learnt to sit and just be, the co-operative took off. It was to run for nearly twenty-five years.

Monise and I were, in fact, to meet twice more before she died, but we were not to know it then, and we were sad. We sipped our sweet tea in silence and when, seeing that she was shaking a little, I asked how it could be that two women of such different backgrounds and histories could possibly enjoy such friendship, Monise put her bony black hand on my white hand and said, 'Same Jesus, same cross.'

I can see our piano of fingers now.

I drove home in Monise's flip flops. A week later Jack and I were back in England.

What shall we do now, sweetheart?

For the first three months we borrowed a friend's cottage in Somerset until our own house was free from tenants. It was a little semi-detached farm workers' cottage set amid farmlands – though at weekends the lane outside became a rat-run for locals on their way to the local tip. We arrived in early spring when the blackthorn was budding and the steep banks were beginning to green with the promise of new life. Later we would find primroses and celandine, and glimpse between the tree trunks, a mist of wood anemones.

There was something extremely soothing about the quiet colours of the English lanes and the little birds, feathered only, it seemed, in shades of brown, ringing out their joyous evensong. I would watch the silhouette of their beaks opening against the sky, amazed that such piercing sweetness could come from such tiny throats. African colours had been so insistent, somehow – crimson poinsettias, scarlet hibiscus, orange flame trees, purple bougainvilleas – and the birds, with their swirling crests and trailing tails, with their carmine breasts and iridescent rainbow feathers – glorious though they were – couldn't sing at all. They had no melodies, only squawks and splutters, chiming with the cicadas to make up the snap, crackle and pop of the African bush.

At first Jack, being an urbanite, was nervous living in such isolation. He was used to buildings around him. But we slowly grew into the space, and it gave us peace. For those twelve weeks we did almost nothing as we tried to persuade ourselves that his problems were simply due to overwork.

The nearest little town was Yarlingford, a good two miles away, and there we found ourselves perplexed by the choices we had to make just to buy the simplest of things. In Zimbabwe we had grown used to only one make of toothpaste, and two makes of soap powder. There were almost no imported goods and vegetables were strictly seasonal. It was not unusual to go into a little roadside store and find the shelves almost empty. Now we found ourselves wandering down the aisles of the supermarket in a daze. How many types of cleaning fluid did you need, how many brands of cereal? So much choice seemed almost obscene.

To fill our days we took little walks, going a few yards further every time, and I nested, as best I could. We had very little money, so I filled glasses with flowers and leaves picked from the hedgerows. We used to do that as children. In spring Mum would pick the first buds on the trees near our home – hawthorn, chestnut, sycamore and hazel – and put them in a glass above the fireplace to see which came into leaf first. It was always the sticky-buds from the horse chestnut tree that won the race.

Now, in the struggling confusion of Jack's illness, I reverted to those childhood pleasures and found a level of comfort.

Having been away from any television for four years it was fascinating to see how much older all the newsreaders looked. We had a lot to catch up on, and Jack was able to distract himself by watching the sport and listening to the news.

We'd only been back a couple of weeks when he began to experience chest pains. He was diagnosed with mild angina. Of course he was worried, but some of our friends had lived with angina for years and we persuaded ourselves that it was no big deal. Part of me still hoped that all his symptoms were due to some form of exhaustion, and would ease.

Certainly he seemed to gain physical and mental strength. With no work demanding his intellectual energies, he seemed less confused. Slowly he relaxed and was in good spirits when the time came for us finally to move back to our own home.

I loved our house. It was a late Georgian semi on the edge of a small market town. I had bought it with borrowed money after I left my first husband. My sister-in-law Ruth had found it for me, and as soon as I walked down the steps into the basement sitting room with its hessian covered walls and its wonderful view down the steep slope of garden, I fell in love with it. I didn't even go upstairs before I made an offer, so it wasn't until I'd moved in that I realised the bedrooms on the third floor were painted bright purple.

I had always felt this house to be a gift from God. I had no money when I left my first marriage, but my mother forked out from her savings and a complete stranger came up to me in the church where I'd met Jack and said, 'God has told me to give you £5,000. Is that all right?' All right! All I needed then was a suitable mortgage, but the Chelsea Building Society, with whom my ex had been saving for some twenty years, finally in our joint names, said I didn't qualify. I decided to appeal and made an appointment with a manager at their central office in London. I took with me a pot of homemade marmalade. This I presented to him, along with my case. I shall never forget this dear man. I was, at this time, rather wan, having just recovered from an operation to remove my appendix along with the accompanying gangrene. Whether it was my state of health, my story – I told him about the £5,000 – or the marmalade, I shall never know. But he granted me a mortgage and wished me well. I had met Jack, by this time, and he helped me decorate the six little rooms which eventually became our marital home.

So here we were, back in it once again. It was strange to walk down the front path after so many years abroad. Our tenants had left the house a uniform beige having re-painted the white woodwork magnolia in an attempt to disguise the tobacco smoke that had discoloured all the wallpapers and curtains.

They also left our address with a supplier of hardcore porn and I spent some months returning plain brown envelopes 'to sender'. (Though I have to say, some of the pictures were quite astonishing.)

But it was good, very good, to be back. The street hadn't changed at all. Except that there was now only one corner shop. The greengrocers, after a short metamorphosis into a lawnmower hire shop, had transmogrified into a funny little house where a single father sat by the front window on a Saturday morning pairing a huge basket-load of clean socks. He only had two children, but I often wondered how many feet they had between them.

Old friends and neighbours welcomed us back with a casual friendliness as though we'd only been away for a holiday instead of six years. Nobody seemed to have changed much. Ellen was looking a little more frail. She had been a tweeny maid to one of the last big families at the top end of the street. She was fourteen then. Now she was in her late seventies, at least, with a white pudding-basin bob. She'd developed a strange lurching walk, her body bent forward as if head-butting a gale force wind.

Fred was still running the remaining corner shop, though his top dentures seemed even less secure – especially when he laughed. When I had first moved into the street, ten years before, the shop was still run like something out of *Lark Rise to Candleford*. Fred sold sherry from wooden casks on the counter and you took your old bottles in to be filled up. The sherry, however, was not as concentrated as his glance – especially once he knew you were a Woman On Your Own.

'I'm advertising for a wife', he had announced seriously one day, the two little hairs on his Adam's apple wobbling up and down above the blue nylon of his overall collar. 'I put an ad in the *Evening Standard*. I was thinking perhaps I could come over this evening and show you the replies?'

It sounds so silly now, but I had panicked. I'd only just left my first husband and hadn't been in the street more than a few weeks. The last thing I wanted was to have to fend off the advances of some randy old man with false teeth.

I rushed round to my neighbour whose son, Harry, was a plumber.

'Mary, Mary, Fred's coming round in half an hour to show me his ads. He says he's looking for a wife.'

Mary's eyes glinted behind the smear of her glasses. Mary's glasses were always covered in a soft film of mud and/or cooking grease, she being both a great gardener and a great cook, but oblivious to dirt.

'HARRY!' she yelled up the stairs. 'To Rebecca's. NOW!' Harry, with long suffering good nature, accompanied me home, and by the time Fred was sitting at my kitchen table with his clutch of 'replies' was upstairs tapping vigorously on the radiators with his hammer, sounding very busy, and very much at hand. Poor Harry. He had to tap away for nearly half an hour, but it got rid of Fred quicker than expected and gave us all a good laugh over a drink that night.

Late-night drinks with Mary became a bit of a ritual. She was a great one for giving her visitors cocoa – with a capful of rum in it when she thought we looked tired. Her basement kitchen was the hub of the street. It was an Aladdin's cave of epicurean delights. Trays of cupcakes for some local bazaar would perch precariously on a sideboard with potted cheeses and a half-eaten pie. Potatoes and marrows from the garden overflowed from wicker baskets. Flagons of homemade wine were brewed under the kitchen table and sat there among the bowls of congealed cat food, the gentle plop-plop of the fermenting yeast accompanying the hiss of the gas stove which always had one ring alight. To this she would turn, every half hour or so, to light another cigarette.

She never stopped cooking – cakes, biscuits, pâtés, rabbit stews. The draining board was crammed with rows of jams and chutneys in various stages of production and potting. Since the cigarette never left her mouth we assumed that ash was an inevitable ingredient of most of her meals which, despite appearances, were always outstanding. She told me once she used to make her own mincemeat, with real meat, hanging it in strips by the door to dry. She was the only person I ever met who could stuff a pillow with real feathers. No one left Mary's kitchen empty-handed. You always had a cake wrapped up in a piece of cling film, or a fistful of runner beans, or a pot of the latest ash jam.

We hadn't been back home more than six months when Jack had a fit. Luckily he was sitting down when it happened, but his pupils grew enormous and he began to dribble as he lost consciousness. I propped him up and held him until the moment passed. He sat in silence, looking bemused, but he didn't complain.

I had been convinced for some time now that Jack wasn't just suffering from exhaustion. Something else was very wrong. A friend had noticed that his right foot was beginning to drag, and now and then I had felt a faint tremor in his arm. And although he was not as stressed as before, he was lack-lustre somehow. Mentally dull. I went to our doctor, a dear man, but on the point of retirement, and told him I was not leaving the surgery until he'd arranged for Jack to see a specialist.

In the end it didn't take long and the diagnosis was fairly swift. Parkinson's. What a relief. At last we knew what we were up against. We knew it was nasty. We knew it could only be slowed down, but not cured, but Jack was by now in his mid-sixties: with luck, and intelligent drug control, his mental impairment would improve and we'd have some good years ahead of us still. We didn't tell anyone but the family – and Mary. We hoped to keep it to ourselves for a bit. But Mary was all for getting people together and to my amazement one day, Nellie Boyd, who lived over the road and was a Strict and Particular Baptist, came tip-toeing to our kitchen door, her thin brown hair coiled round her head in a plait like a little rat's tail. She hovered a moment.

'May I come in? I don't mean to intrude. I hope you don't mind. We heard about your news. My husband has Parkinson's and we're members of the Parkinson's Society. We would love to help you if we can. Would you like to join?' And she placed on the kitchen table all the ghastly details.

We didn't want to join. We didn't want our lives to be defined by Jack's illness. He was more than just a man with not enough dopamine. But Nellie turned out to be a wonderful ally, and full of surprises. We would meet in the street and compare notes.

'Were you kicked out of bed last night?' I'd ask – one of the symptoms of Parkinson's being strong leg jerks that knocked the hell out of your sleep patterns.

'Not quite,' she'd say, a shy smile trembling the soft hair on her cheeks, 'but you've got to snuggle up close, haven't you, no matter what. There's nothing like bed, is there? It's the best bit of the day.' Not overly strict then, I thought. Over the next few years we bumped into each other on the pavement and buoyed each other up with little anecdotes. She had a surprising capacity for laughter.

And so Jack and I struggled on. For the first five or so years we managed well enough. At least to begin with. Knowing he had something recognisably wrong was a huge relief to him, and at first the pills had seemed to work. His mental reactions speeded up a little and, contrary to expectations, his physical symptoms were not very noticeable. We still held the odd meeting at home. Very odd in the case of the Liberal Democrats because Fred Jenkins insisted on bringing his ferret, which he kept in his trouser pocket. Jack would have nothing to do with these evenings and I was never sure if it was because of the politics or the smell.

For the first few years he was able to read, and to write and paint a little, though it distressed him that he could no longer concentrate to study. He was asked to preach now and then, but he couldn't summon his thoughts. In the end he gave up, and that's when I noticed that he had stopped laughing. It was as if a darkness was gathering around him. Every now and then a spark would break out and he would light up – but only every now and then, and only for a moment.

We still went for walks, though they got shorter and slower. We used to take Mum, who liked to 'stride out' – even though she was in her eighties – her white stick tap tapping the road, her conversation relentlessly bold. I loved her walker's gait, the way she thrust forward, nose first, even though she could barely see, wanting to know what was in the hedgerows, and could we find a violet, or a primrose, or autumn berries for her room. She was exhausting. Wonderful in retrospect, but exhausting.

While Mum relished these walks, Jack merely allowed himself to be taken along. It was a way to kill time, a diversion, though increasingly difficult as it became harder for him to lift his feet from the ground. What he really wanted to do was come alive again. I would find myself dawdling between the two of them, trying to keep the conversation going, since Jack barely spoke, trying, for my own sake, to enjoy the sights and sounds of our country lanes. I was determined to live positively within our diminishing space, because diminishing it was.

I had been working on a new biography, but abandoned it as leaving Jack alone became too problematical. I was able to take local work, just to get out a bit, and neighbours and friends drifted in and out of the house, as usual, their chatter and laughter hiding the silences. Those only came once the back door was closed. Jack hid his depression well in company, but it was grinding him down, and when everyone had gone I would hold him close, hoping the physical touch would ease his mental pain.

But something more than depression was happening to his mind. At first I just noticed little things. I was watching him one morning and it became clear that although he was holding the paper in front of his face, and turning the pages, he wasn't actually reading. He was just looking at the print and moving his head from side to side. He behaved as though this was quite normal.

Another day I found him sitting at the kitchen table, his back very straight, as usual. He was wearing the Clothkit jerkin I had made him years before. His hand, holding a pen, was poised immobile over some writing paper. I saw tears on his face.

'I want to write to my son,' he whispered, 'but I can't remember how to do it.'

Worst of all was his increasing silence. He who had been so free and easy with words, whose prose was like poetry, who could voice the inexpressible, was now finding it increasingly difficult to speak in sentences, or to process what you were saying to him. Some days he would spend just sitting on the sofa, staring at nothing, as though he'd been stunned, traumatised by the changes in his abilities which, with one part of his mind, he saw so clearly. It was as if his brain was cut in half. One half was shutting down, the other was looking at it, aware of what was happening, but unable to know how to stop it.

On better days he would follow me from room to room, looking bewildered, and repeating with a barely concealed desperation, 'What shall we do now, sweetheart? What shall we do now?' And I would try to find little tasks for him to do that would pass the time, that he could accomplish without muddle, in some effort to restore his self-confidence.

I was amazed by the sweetness with which he bore all this grief. For me one of the most painful aspects of his suffering was the patience with which he bore it. It tore my heart out.

I knew he was weeping inside out of boredom and bewilderment, trapped by limitations that he couldn't understand. Yet despite all this disintegration there was something at the core of this man of mine that never changed, that remained completely intact.

Then new symptoms appeared. Periods of terrible pain, which nothing seemed to alleviate. His nerve ends felt 'on fire'. Night after night went by when he couldn't sleep, and I would lie beside him, rubbing his back, hour after hour, murmuring him into drowsiness in the moments of respite.

Secretly, I was sure that he didn't have simple Parkinson's. Something else was wrong. What were these periods of unexplained pain, or the times he lost control of his bodily functions, his bowels suddenly giving way? The strange little faints? And then there was the dramatic but spasmodic loss of his intellectual powers. He would sit for hours in an almost catatonic state, and then emerge apparently normal, able to hold a conversation, albeit haltingly, and – more significantly – be able to pick up on emotional undercurrents and tensions.

On these occasions he would ask, rather crossly, why I was so stressed? What was the matter with me? It was as though he'd been on another planet for hours, or days, or weeks even, and then suddenly returned to earth. But earth was not as he had left it.

What he couldn't understand – and what I was desperately trying to hide from him – was that as his own life diminished, so did my own. It grew narrower and narrower, focused almost entirely on his well-being. He turned to me for spiritual sustenance as his own sense of God slowly ebbed away. He turned to me for laughter, because he could not make his own. He turned to me for physical comfort and I poured my life into his, because he was my lover, my man. 'What shall we do now, sweetheart? What shall we do now?' Oh God, I don't know. Don't ask me. Don't ask me. For God's sake, don't keep asking me.

My brother Michael fixed for us to see a colleague of his at University College Hospital. Pranesh Talwar had a reputation for being a brilliant neurologist. Michael had the deepest regard for him as a person, as well as a doctor. Jack's new GP was a friend of ours, a very clever diagnostician in his own right, but he too was perplexed by the new developments. We went to UCH with his blessing.

It was a surprising visit. I'd been there many times before. Michael had trained at the hospital, and was now a consultant, and all our family had been treated there, over the years. We were sitting in the scruffy little waiting corridor, me thumbing through tatty copies of the *Mail on Sunday* when a tall figure, stooping a little from the shoulders, opened a consulting-room door. There was something very still about him, almost as if he was watching from the shadows. He spoke a name and as he did so an elderly man got up and began to shuffle towards him. He looked a complete wreck. His clothes were filthy, his hair was unkempt, and it was clear from the way he moved that he couldn't lift up his feet. But I shall never forget the way that consultant looked at him. He took in the man's whole person, from top to toe, and his gaze clothed him with dignity. Please God, let this be Pranesh Talwar. And it was.

Being from Pakistan he knew about cricket, and he and Jack talked boy talk for a while. I could see the old spark of communication light up in Jack's face. His speech was halting, but his eyes were bright. Together we chatted about all sorts of unexpected things, from politics to belief systems, before he examined Jack briefly and it was agreed that he should return to hospital for three days of extensive tests.

There was something about Pranesh that made both of us feel safe, as if the chaos we were beginning to experience could be kept within bounds, as if somehow, whatever it turned out to be, it would be manageable. More than that, he had an ability to communicate on many levels and we felt that Jack was being seen as a whole person, not merely as a body with symptoms, or a person in crisis. Pranesh didn't minimise us, and he gave of himself. He was professional but he was not aloof. Maybe knowing Michael helped to make the meeting more relaxed than it might otherwise have been. We had a family connection. But I suspect he was like that with everyone.

Before we left I told him I wanted to know the bottom line, whatever it was. I wanted to know exactly what Jack and I had to face.

The following week I took Jack back, settling him in the ward, and for the first time in literally years, had three whole days to myself. What bliss. One of the worst things over the last few years had been that I had no private time or space in which to grieve without Jack noticing. Despite everything he could still sense my moods. And he followed me everywhere. There was nowhere to hide. But I needed to mourn – I needed to cry for the loss of my man, for the pain of his suffering, for the loss of my own creative life. Yet now I had the freedom to do so, I couldn't. I'd spent so much time disguising my emotions that I'd become emotionally constipated. But I knew that in these three days I had to make myself cry, to find a way to release the feelings that were building up inside.

It was José Carreras who did the trick. One evening I found a CD of him singing the Creole Mass. It was an early recording and the tenderness of his young voice was piercing. I wept. I wept as loudly as I could so that I could hear myself weep. I wanted the sound to fill the room. I wanted it to reverberate off the walls, to bounce back and hit me. For some reason it seemed really important that I registered to myself that I was weeping. I wept until my body and my voice were exhausted. And then I had a large glass of vodka. From that day onwards, if I needed to release tears, I would listen to Carreras.

On the day I went to collect Jack from the hospital I asked to see Pranesh on my own.

'Come to my room,' he said, and led me through what seemed an endless labyrinth of corridors – cream walls spotted with brown doors. I wanted to talk on the way, to burst out with, 'What is it? Have you found out what is wrong with Jack? Can you help him? Please tell me,' but Pranesh walked steadily in front of me and I could sense his determination not to speak until we were seated. The anxiety bubbled up like fizz in my chest.

When we were seated he began.

'Rebecca, we think Jack has something called Diffuse Cortical Lewy Body Disease. We're getting more subtle in our understanding of brain diseases, and this is still quite new to us, but I'm pretty sure this is what he has. The physical symptoms are not unlike Parkinson's, but not usually quite so severe, which is why sometimes it's misdiagnosed, but instead of just part of the brain being affected, a large area of his brain is affected. The cortex, the outside layer of his brain, is actually shrinking.'

I didn't know what to make of it. 'Will it be like Alzheimer's? Will he not know me? Will he become violent? Will he know what's happening?'

'It's not like Alzheimer's. He is likely to dip in and out of dementia. He's a gentle man, isn't he, and I think he will remain gentle. It will be slow, as if his brain is quietly closing down. And it could take many years, we just don't know. He will just gradually lose his faculties. He's probably been showing symptoms for some time now, but until it got to this stage, you might not have noticed. There's nothing we can do except try to support you both and help you find ways to manage it.'

'But what about the pain?'

'We don't really know what that is. All we can do is try to alleviate it.'

Pranesh sat very still. I could see why he and my brother got on so well, they both seemed to have a depth they could move into when things were tough. His calmness gave me courage. It was as if, without putting it into words, he was saying, 'You can do this. You'll have the strength to do this.' I remember when my mother knew she was going blind, Michael had gone to the hospital with her for the final results and she had said to him, 'Will I go blind, Michael?' and he replied, 'Yes, you will, but you will never be black blind,' and Mum said that gave her courage. She knew the truth, but she knew the limitations of the illness and she knew what she had to face.

I decided then and there that I would never lie to Jack about his condition. He hated what he called charades around death beds. The terminally ill always knew what was happening, and he knew something very serious was wrong. I wouldn't hide that from him, but I would keep the details and the end result to myself. He was, after all, over twenty years my senior, and he could well die of physical frailty before he finally lost all mental functions, so Pranesh and I agreed that we would tell the truth, but not all of the truth. We'd explain that he would not get better, that his symptoms were likely to get worse, but very slowly. In the meantime the doctors would try to control the pain, and he and I would endeavour to live as fully as possible.

Jack seemed peaceful when we left the hospital. He was clearly relieved to have some sort of diagnosis. How much he took in, I don't know, but he didn't seem unduly disturbed, and we held hands that evening and watched the news – very quietly, because any loud sound he would interpret as aggression, even when it was laughter.

When Jack had gone to bed and I could be alone at last, I stood at the foot of the stairs and howled. Or rather, I just opened my mouth and no sound came out, like a wolf baying at the moon in a silent movie. I felt as if I had been blown up inside and only my skin was holding me together.

Once I'd picked myself up after the first shock of diagnosis I realised holding it together was going to require more than my skin. I would have to dig deep and find the resources to squeeze out of life all possible joy and delight. Jack and I had always laughed a lot together. We laughed almost as much as we talked. My task, I felt, was to keep that laughter alive.

But how? How would I hide from him the pain of every day? I knew that I had to find some outlet for all the emotions that were threatening to overwhelm me, and I certainly was not going to burden family or friends. I could only think of one release – to write, but to write about all the wonderful quirky people we lived among and who laced their way, with such kindness, through our lives. And I felt, too, that I should monitor just what God was going to do about it all. Where would he be, in all this mess?

PART TWO

Journal

1994

19 June: So now, my love, I know the worst. Your brain is shrinking inside your skull. You are going to disintegrate very slowly, mind and body. You will know what's happening to you. You will see your shit on the floor, on your feet, but you won't know how it got there. You will see me distraught and distorted and know that you have made me so, and not know how to stop it, or how to help. You will feel our loving in rags and your God absent and I will hold you to my breast and cradle the shell of your skull, for you will have gone, my lover, my dear one. But not quite.

But I am with you. I am your wife. We will live through this together. We will see this illness as a journey we take together. I am so afraid of what it will actually mean.

27 July: My birthday. I'm forty-nine. It's great having the corner shop literally over the road. Big John, who lives a few houses down and mans the till sometimes, when he's bored, helped me blow up balloons. We tied them to the railings. Some popped and Lizzie, next door, heard the bang and stuck her head cautiously out of her basement window. 'Excuse me,' she stammered, 'excuse me, is anybody there?'

'It's only my balloons, Liz.'

'Oh. Oh, good. I thought it was gunshot.' And back in darted her little crinkled tortoise head, all nose and scales with the dried dead skin of oldness. She has lived next door for over fifty years and still remembers the war.

Jack was semi-comatose all day, but the street dropped in and out with flowers and birthday greetings. He woke up this evening. Old friends called round and talked about their work. Jack and I both go into a sort of mourning when this happens. We sit on the sidelines of life, longing to be involved. He stopped me talking. He said I talked too much. He can barely talk at all now. It makes him feel marginalised. He's always been the speaker, the up-front man. Now he sits in this straitjacket of silence, unable to think fast enough to join in. Unable, so often, even to find the words.

But these visits also make him see how I am dying here beside him. He can't bear the pain of that. I love him and so I must not die. The parameters of our life may be shrinking, but I am determined to live creatively within this narrowing space. I promise you I will not let your illness destroy me. You are my rock. You woke me on our wedding night and stroked the salt on my face. 'Don't cry, sweetheart,' you said. 'It's over now. Those days are over now.' And I curled round your warm skinny body and thought how much more committed and precious than sex was this intimacy of the night, when, deep in our belonging, we held each other safe against the rest of the world. Safe at last from the bathroom door that my father opened when I was pubescent and should have been left alone, and the bedroom door that opened as Mother slunk to my bedside to weep and warn and wring her hands. Safe from the cruelty of my first marriage, from that tongue that slashed away until I didn't know who I was any more, or even if I existed at all until I hit my shin on the coffee table one afternoon and thought, 'so I am still here'. That was not a good marriage. My first. Not only did I lose all sense of personal identity, I lost God.

Living in the country, I had grown up with a mystical sense of the divine. God had been immanent to me in the wind and the waves, particularly the wind. As a child I would climb to the top of the sycamore tree in my two-button jacket and hand-me-down trousers (they were brown cord, with knee patches, I loved them), and there, high above the world – and far from the smirks of my brother – I would sing out my wordless paeans to the wild sky. I was quite sure that if I stretched my arms out high enough, my whole being would be gathered up into the light. I felt wonderfully free.

Not for long, as it happened. When I was eleven my mother, egged on by the local priest for whom she had a barely concealed tenderness, deemed it time for me to go to confession and dwell on my wickedness. My wickedness, it appeared, resided largely in my bottom, which my mother corseted at an early age because 'all the men are looking at you.' Since I only weighed seven stone, there can't have been that much to look at. But that, really, put paid to the sky. As Adam bit on the apple and tasted sin, so I bit on the holy wafer and tasted guilt. The accusing wine of the blood of Christ began to flow through my veins, helped on its way by my mother's intrusive gaze. My pre-teenage years were now jagged with twin horrors: I was either going to have a baby before I was married, or I was going to become a nun. I used to lie in the bath and wiggle my big toe under the dripping tap, whispering 'I will. I won't. I will. I won't.' If a drip fell on my toe it meant I definitely was going to have a baby. If it didn't, I was safe. For today. Prayers by the side of the bed: 'Thank you, God. But please don't let me be a nun.'

Wriggling, somehow, out of both the corsets and the confessional, I turned instead to the village church, largely because Marty, my first boyfriend whom I had met at a village dance, was low Anglican and not too keen on confession. He had eyes the colour of burnt caramel and knew the call of every bird. For a while we walked together across the fields to Evensong, the bells tolling out to chivvy us on. Sometimes he would touch my breasts, but not often enough. I loved the summer, especially when the hedgerows were a ramshackle of briars, the dog roses barely pink. Then winter came.

One year followed another and I lived my life through a series of boyfriends, some of whom I liked. I had begun training on a local paper and was doing well, my initial six months' probation cut short because most of it was spent carrying double trays of tea to the reporters and subs and I was finally deemed too small to stagger round with them. By this time Michael had left home to go to medical school, cutting the umbilical cord on the way, leaving mother adrift. Now she only had me.

They used to say of my mother that when she was a young woman she would walk through the door and her presence would light up the room. By the time Dad had left forever, and I was in my late teens, that light had turned to a bitter darkness. My friends were now going to college and moving away, or having love affairs and moving away, but I remained, tied by a terrible sense of pity to my mother's side. Once I tried to leave, to share a flat with a girlfriend in London, but she primed the neighbours to accuse me of selfishness. I still remember the woman down the road who was married to an inventor. He had removed their staircase the previous year and they had to climb upstairs on a ladder. She was six months pregnant. She walked into our sitting room one day and asked how I could be so cruel as to leave my mother. I was twenty-one.

I didn't leave, but mainly because I had nowhere to go to, and no one to go with. And how could I step out alone, into such a threateningly empty space? On days off work I would still walk the fields, but turning for home, I would linger, walking round the block again and again, day dreaming of a different future – though I found it hard to picture one – putting off the moment when I had to open the front gate and walk towards the front door. As the gate clicked shut behind me I felt bowed down by duty, as if I was dragging myself behind me, dropping my heart like a stone.

So the God of my childhood became first my accuser and then my taskmaster, and I wrapped myself not in the wind, but in ritual. And words. Words, words, words. The words of the Psalms, the words of the Creed, the words of the Confession, the words of the Absolution. It was words that trapped most of the spiritual life in the Christian church I grew up in, strangling spiritual imagination, destroying innocence, boxing the divine into a tomb of concrete formulas. But they put a framework around the void, so words became my barrier against the nothing. And I clung to them all. Until.

I can remember with absolute clarity the time and the place, the very moment I realised that we had all been lied to, that all those words were false. It was a dull November day. I had finally managed to wrench myself free from home. I had met a man who read a lot of books, and married him. He was very clever and surprisingly good to Mum. His name was Paul and he had a tongue like a razor blade, cleverly hidden behind a brilliant wit most frequently aimed at my housewifely ineptitude. Paul and I had married probably because we were both fed up with being virgins and his initial tenderness and attention – punctuated as it had been at times by moments of amused irritation – had turned, virtually overnight, into perpetual scorn.

Why I should suddenly, after a fairly normal, if short, courtship, irritate him so relentlessly, I was too immature to understand. He was a little older than me, and I had been excited by his intelligence and the extent of his library – not to mention his wine cellar. I should have realised things might become difficult when he cancelled our honeymoon just before the wedding and spent the first week of our marriage putting six layers of polyurethane on a dining-room table he had constructed from old planks of wood, getting up at regular intervals during the night to check it out. But why didn't I fight back? Argue? Have a point of view? As it was I couldn't understand why everything I said was contradicted and why I so obviously drove him mad. The most public sign of his prolonged irritation was when, one spring, I broke the teeth of his green comb in the bathroom and the following Christmas, which we spent with friends, his only present to me, carefully wrapped, was a new plastic comb. Green.

Eventually I was to understand that it was all about control. The traumas of his childhood meant that unless he could control everything and everyone around him, he felt his world was disintegrating. But at the time I didn't have the psychological insight to understand him or bring out the best in him. Luckily, many years later, a more discerning woman than I made a better job of it.

But anyway, here I was, at twenty-three, living in Liverpool with my irascible husband, looking out of the top-floor window of our home, utterly bemused by the emotional turmoil in which I found myself. In the near distance the River Mersey drudged its way towards the sea. The drizzle was as thick as mist and there seemed to be no differentiation between earth and sky. I remember thinking, 'The sky is falling down'. I had been married almost a year and for most of that year had been calling out to a God who never answered. No matter what words I used, what rituals I obeyed, no matter what cleric I talked to, what books I read, I simply could not find the key to unlock the silence. And then, like the early mists clearing before the morning sun, I suddenly saw clearly. I remember the moment as if it were yesterday. I knew, quietly, and without any doubt, the reason why. There was nothing there. There was no God.

Ten years of silence followed, though I never quite stopped listening. We had moved from Merseyside to a soul-destroying suburban sprawl of concrete and pebbledash in Outer London and were surviving each other on a diet of non-communication and fine wines. Or rather he was. I was not surviving. I was later told that you could divide humanity roughly in two – those who gave nervous breakdowns and those who had them.

I had seen an ad in the local paper about a workshop on prayer, to be run by the Reverend Jack McGuire. I was frantically trying to find some sort of inner equilibrium, and in a final shout of desperation called out to the empty air, 'OK, I'll go, but God, if you do exist – be there.'

And there he was. Not remotely like God, with his purple pocket-handkerchief and shock of white hair. His vitality was electric. He seemed to burn up the atmosphere, sparking it with laughter and throwing out, so apparently casually, the most astonishing possibilities as he talked in terms I had never heard before about a God I didn't recognise. He made it seem possible that this God was both real, and approachable – and more than that, exciting.

His jokes were clearly tried and tested, but everyone was so relaxed. There was a sense not just of expectation, but of easy enjoyment, as if the God they were all talking about was knowable, fun to be with. Could that possibly be true? The God of my childhood had been conspicuously absent for so long by then, and no grown-up God had matured to take his place, that it seemed impossible to me that people with minds could still believe in a God at all. Yet here they were. And here was I. And there was Jack.

It was then, that first evening, that I recognised him. Some might call it falling in love, but it wasn't quite that. It was simply – recognition. We were part of the same whole. That was it. Recognising God took a little longer. But after many more months of intellectual struggle, I did. And of course, in the end, it was not my mind that was finally convinced, but my heart, or rather, my whole being. Just as once I had known without doubt that God did not exist, so one day I knew that God did.

I remember the moment so clearly. I was sitting in my study one evening, trying to work out how to pray, when I was suddenly overwhelmed by what I can only describe as a joyous sense of the divine. It utterly engulfed me. It filled every part of me. It could not be denied. I felt connected, creature to Creator, as if a pathway had opened up between us. It was incredibly exciting. It was utter delight. And I was free again. From that moment on I experienced again that personal connection with the divine that had been the core of my childhood spirituality, uncontaminated by theology. Gone was the sense of duty, of guilt needing to be absolved, of rules to be obeyed, feelings that had so corrupted those early years. There was only a sense of being utterly loved and accepted, of being re-connected with the source of all that was creative, and hopeful and restorative. It was healing, unconditional love.

Of course, as I began to live the life, theology re-emerged. It became the scaffolding upon which I lived my life until, many, many years later, I had once again to cut myself free, and start again in a wordless place. But that was for the future. For the now, I was caught, hook, line and sinker, and it was utterly liberating.

Many months after that first encounter with Jack, as I lay motionless, trying to take up as little space in the bed as possible, trying not to touch my husband lest I should trigger some unwanted response, I had a dream. I dreamt that Jack had taken my face in his hand, and, for a moment, held it. I awoke that morning overwhelmed by the tenderness of his touch. I knew that in real life he would never touch me – I was someone else's wife, I don't think it would even have crossed his mind – but in that moment I realised I would rather live alone, however scary that was to me, than continue to live without love. That morning I packed my bags and left. Three hours later I was in my brother's house watching Ruth, my sister-in-law, breastfeed the baby at the kitchen table, a row of nappies drying on the line above the stove. She had greeted me with her usual welcoming smile. 'The spare room's all yours, for as long as you want it,' she said. I stayed ten months, and filed for divorce.

But for Jack there had been no such sense of connection, no such premonition of love. Later he told me that often that year, when his front door closed at night, his last meeting over, he would wander into the bedroom, and opening the cupboard doors, bury his face in the clothes of his dead wife.

14 August: Had Mum round for lunch, she in full bloom, her small bosom (in new corset) thrust forward. At one point, apropos of nothing, except that there was a lull in the conversation, she threw back her head, and with the knuckles of her right hand brushing her fevered brow in a brief, upward sweep, sighed, 'Ah well. Hail and Farewell.' I'm not sure, but I think she might have been talking about the Cruelty and Transience of Life. Meanwhile Jack is bravely trying not to faint in the next room as I hold him up, legs sagging, arms beginning to flail. I'm supposed to lie him on the floor when he has one of these turns, but if I do, I can't get him up again. So I sit him down and walk in a 'measured rush' between Mum and Jack, trying to cope with both. I notice I have my Joyce Grenfell voice on again…

15 August: Jack very poorly. I comfort him the best I can through the night, stroking his back and talking gently. Sometimes I sing snatches of the folk songs that he likes which lull him into a doze. The doc gave him painkillers which drugged him so much he couldn't speak or walk, but didn't touch the pain. He is at the end of his tether. Quite apart from the physical symptoms, his depression and anxiety seem to deepen every day. I don't like to leave him for more than a few minutes on his own. If I do he follows me from room to room, seeking a comfort I cannot give him. I try to stay very close and touch him as much as I can.

We had an emergency appointment with Pranesh Talwar on Thursday and he's trying out a new drug regime to see if it helps the pain. It seems to be working. My own doc has put me on 2mg of amitriptyline at night because it has the effect of helping the brain to switch off again. Even on nights when Jack is able to sleep we are usually up two or three times because he's so anxious about going to the bathroom, and he can no longer walk there by himself. We are both exhausted. It's been a dreadful week.

To cap it all Mum is now finding it difficult to cope on her own. She has such spirit. She's been determined to keep her independence, but she can only see outlines now, so I'm cooking for her and taking weekly supplies for her to freeze – a different meal for each evening. It takes nearly an hour to drive to her flat, which is a good 30 miles away down the M25, and I have to bundle Jack in and out of the car and hoist him up her steep stairs. I know she appreciates it, but she still can't help herself complaining: 'Oh, Rebecca, I do get rather tired of your cheese sauces.'

She's a strange mixture of love and jealousy, my Mum. I often wonder what went wrong. Her old friend Irene, now 91, with all her grey cells intact (she still reads the *Guardian* cover to cover) but only a single tooth in each corner, told me the other day that when she was young Mum's presence was radiant. 'Becca', she said, leaning towards me, lisping through her gaps, 'your mother could make a simple supper feel like a feast.'

When my brother Michael and I were very small she would sit by our beds and sing us to sleep with the soft lilting folk songs that spoke of love and lost love. We didn't know then that she sang, not for us alone. Poor Mum. I think the heart of it was that she could never forgive Dad for his wartime infidelities. The tragedy of my parents is that they so nearly made it.

We always knew when Dad was home because you could smell his tobacco at the garden gate. It was Balkan Sobranie. On Sunday afternoons the cat and I would curl up on his lap while he smoked his pipe and read Penguin detective stories in green and white covers, his stubby fingers stroking first the cat's ear, and then mine, in an absent-minded affection, until one or other of us wriggled too much and he let us go in a tumbling indignity of fur and limbs.

I only remember Mum and Dad hugging once, in the hall beside the grandfather clock, and I stood outside them and embraced them both – trying to bond them together, I suppose. I was about seven.

The thing I remember most about being seven was that I had a small red second-hand bicycle that the Johnson boys – who lived opposite and whose father Drank and Had Women – threw out of their bedroom window. I had stood outside the house gazing up in fascinated horror as, with a raucous shout, they had hurled my precious bike out of the top floor. I remember they'd had a struggle getting it through the bedroom window. But it was only small, and so was I. It fell with a sort of bounce. They were spanked for that, which was some compensation for the bent front mudguard.

But the violence of the assault, not on my bike, but on my imagination, passed unnoticed.

I mostly remember Dad as being away, but he always returned for Christmas. We brought out the wine glasses and the white damask napkins in their silver rings. He would say grace with his hands folded, fingers interlocked on the table in front of him. 'Benedictus, benedicat.' We didn't know what it meant, but it was mercifully short, and the food was getting cold.

'I don't want much,' he used to murmur with his nonchalant French pout, 'just a little skin and bones,' and onto his plate he would carefully pile the crunchy skin, the juicy slivers of dark meat that lingered after the carving, and huge turkey bones still heavily fleshed. On the periphery he spooned the sprouts with chestnuts cooked in milk, the roast potatoes, stuffings and gravy. Into this vast edifice he picked delicately and silently away. He dined with great finesse, sipping his wine and wiping the grease marks from the rim of the glass with his thumb. Half an hour later, hands neatly folded once more, he would sit with a straight back and the utmost dignity before his empty plate.

Boxing Day was his favourite. He would take all day to make a special bolognese sauce on the Aga. This was still in the days of rationing and such food was strangely foreign and extravagant then in an England which hadn't yet learnt the joys of international cuisine. I remember it had strips of belly pork, garlic, tomatoes, herbs and onions, and a dab or two of wine and every half hour or so he'd go to the pot and stir with his strong hands, and then lick the wooden spoon.

When it was ready, he would comfy himself in the big armchair as the afternoon wintered in, tuck a huge white napkin under his chin so that it flowed copiously over the vastness of his stomach, and perch upon it a vegetable dish full of spaghetti. 'All is safely gathered in,' winked Mother, after each delicate twirl of the fork had pitched a haystack of pasta into his slightly greasy, opening mouth.

Father took his pleasures with a strange delicacy – but he took them, which was Mum's complaint really. We lived in the invisible presence of unforgiveness, of unresolved guilt, which formed the groundswell of our lives then, and for ever afterwards. Not that I expect there were many pleasures really. Just a few, taken to ease the bleak journey homewards. Except there wasn't really a home for Dad. To live unforgiven is not to have a home. Nowhere safe to rest your head.

'Dear Uncle Andrew, thang you very muck the prensit...' so, invariably, started my childhood Christmas thank you letters. Dear Dad, thank you for stroking my ear. Don't worry about the rest. I understand all that now. Sorry I never answered your letters. Or not many. But you know I loved you. I think I told you so. It's just that you left – not that I blame you one bit. And when you did return, the look you gave me was not fatherly.

19 August: I don't want to let J's illness, or Mum's increasing demands, overwhelm me. Struggling to remain myself. It's becoming increasingly difficult as one activity after another has to be curtailed, either because Jack needs me, or I'm too tired to do them. Feel as if I'm in a battle for survival. It would be easy in a way to give in, to become submerged. But I'm too selfish to let that happen. I'm desperate to survive.

Sunday 21 August: Feel very depressed. I felt so afraid the other day, and wanted out. I didn't know how to go through with the future, but the words of Christ in Gethsemane came to me loud and clear. He too yearned to escape, even from the thing he most wanted in love and obedience to do. My own faith feels grim, but grounded. I feel like someone halfway up a steep cliff, clinging to the rock face in the teeth of a gale. No one mentioned the power of the wind in Gethsemane.

Ours is a God incarnate into suffering. There would be no excuse for him if he were not.

25 August: Still feeling very depressed. How long will this go on? One year, two years – five years from now? The thing is, I have forgotten what Jack was like when he was well. This is a terrible distress. Feel I am sleepwalking and every now and then wake up to find I'm in a nightmare.

1 September: I am experimenting with 'micro-living'. Since I too, am becoming housebound with Jack, I have been trying to find a way to enjoy our world-in-the-small and not feel so trapped. My brother and I were born on Exmoor and our family roots go back there for as far as we can trace them. We're part of the Doones and the Ridds. I have a picture of my Great-great-aunt Ridd in a locket. She is wearing a formidable bonnet.

My desire to see Devon again is so intense sometimes, it's like a physical pain. But that's not going to happen while Jack is alive, so I decided I had to find my own little patch of wildness here, in my narrow garden. What I had to do was concentrate on what was around me, focusing on the detail and cutting out all the negative stuff that surrounds it. So today I trained our binoculars on the little viburnum tree outside our French doors. I've hung this tree with fat balls, niger seeds, sunflower seeds and peanuts, and slowly, over the last couple of months, an astonishing range of little birds has come to feast – birds I didn't know were living here: bullfinch, goldfinch and chaffinch, a sweet little brownish-green job I've identified as a siskin. The wrens are back, though they stick to the fences, and I was thrilled to see a flock of coal tits and several blackcaps. And hopping on the ground, his breast as bold as a zebra, was a male mistle thrush.

I try to look intently, to relish each detail – the different shapes of their beaks, the intricacies of their feathers, the way they squabble and hop and lilt from branch to branch. I'd been brought up to dislike starlings – but they are beautiful, iridescent and dotted with light. They squawk a bit, that's true, but don't we all. I've counted fourteen varieties of birds so far. The blue tits are so greedy, they're more like flying peanuts than birds. And then I watch our two black cats slowly hunching up the garden, bellies low, turning our wild flowerbeds into the Serengeti as they stalk their prey. The only problem is that Olive (so named because when she was a kitten she looked good enough to eat) is so fat that the earth shakes when she moves and she never fails to look bewildered when the birds calmly fly away when she gets too near. They always leave it to the last minute. Maybe they sense the final pounce will be just a little too tricky for her.

Sometimes I'm too tired to look so intensely, but I find that by stopping in my tracks, just now and then, and saying out loud to myself, 'This moment is lovely, these buds are beautiful, this air feels good ...' helps me to believe that life is not passing me by, that I have what is needed to stimulate the soul here around me, if only I can learn to cut out the intrusions – the noise of neighbours and traffic, Jack's suffering, the insistent domestic chores – and somehow hone in on the small details so that, if only for a moment, they are all that matters.

Well, that's the theory. Half the time I'm too knackered, and a glass of wine and some bollocks on the telly seem an easier solution.

Saturday 3 September: A disturbing thing happened today. Last week, a guy called Nicholas rang me. I'd only met him once before, at a committee meeting to discuss the street bonfire party. We have one every few years to raise funds for charity and to bring our commuter-fractured community together. He only moved into the road a few months ago but was keen to get stuck in, and he and I were given the task of clearing the site by the park at the back and getting the necessary permissions. He struck me as being rather small and brown. He was wearing sandals, which from my point of view was a bad sign.

'I think we ought to get together to discuss what we're going to do,' he said. 'Perhaps we could chat over lunch?'

'Can we make it the afternoon?' I asked, not having the slightest wish to go to lunch with a man who wore sandals. 'I don't like to leave Jack for too long.'

'Come on, it would do you good to get out,' he said – as if he had the faintest idea about what would do me good. There was something pushy about his manner I didn't like.

'Well, you come here then,' I said. 'We'd be delighted to see you and we can talk business afterwards.'

'No, I'm going to give you lunch.'

I protested, but he went on and on like a wasp buzzing round a picnic table. In the end I gave in and said OK. Jack was having a goodish day, and seemed happy to be left, and so off I went. I got back about four hours ago, but I'm still feeling disturbed. Something uncomfortable has happened and I can't quite get rid of it.

He came to pick me up, as planned.

I had assumed we'd just be going to the local pub, but he'd booked a table at a little French restaurant on the edge of town. It was a wild day and we crowded under the umbrella to keep dry. Once in the restaurant, with me trying to make polite conversation – after all I'd only met the guy once before, and had, as far as I could tell, almost nothing in common with him – I had a strong and completely unexpected urge to reach out for his hand. We were waiting to be served and his hand lay on the table just inches from mine – a strong, square hand. I felt exactly as if I was being pulled by a magnet, but while my body seemed to move naturally towards his, my mind was moving fast in the opposite direction. What was all this? I certainly didn't find him attractive, and I wasn't even sure I particularly liked him. His conversation was thin, to say the least, though mercifully he avoided sport, yet despite that, touching him seemed the most natural thing in the world.

I struggled through the meal, trying to get the business done, but he kept stalling. 'We can discuss all that next time'. *Oh no we can't, sunshine. There isn't going to be a next time.* Who was this guy?

When we left, the wind had turned to beating rain. It lashed strands of hair across my face, but the wet didn't seem to bother him. He let me have the umbrella to myself and walked by my side. I realised he was not much taller than me, and he had that little bounce in his step I've noticed in other small men. He reminded me of those birds that hop in the sand by the sea edge, ducking in and out of the waves. As we came to the zebra crossing he put his hand on the nape of my neck, steering me across the road for all the world as if he'd led me thus a thousand times before. And I felt affronted. There was something so presumptuous about that gesture, so possessive – an arrogant assumption that I wouldn't mind. Who the hell did he think he was?

'Rebecca,' he said, when we'd stopped in the shelter of a shop doorway, 'you wait here out of the rain. I'll go and get the car.' And so saying he reached out and brushed the hair from my forehead. 'You're drenched,' he murmured, and there passed over his face a look of such extreme tenderness that it startled me.

To say I felt violated would be completely wrong. His manner and his touch were too gentle for that, but I felt strongly, and I still feel it now, that he had intruded, unbidden, into my very personal space. He was a stranger. He had no business being tender with me. There is also something particularly offensive about flirting with the wife of a disabled man. And yet, he wasn't actually flirting, that's what's so confusing. But I am also shocked by my reactions to him. Why had it felt so easy, so natural, to reach out for his hand, and why had it been such a struggle not to?

Anyway I'm going to forget about him now, but it has thrown me.

4 September: I will not let Jack's illness become a cage. I am determined to live fully in this shrinking space but I long for stimulating company. I am dying inside. I realise that if I am to survive this, and be for Jack the companion he needs, I must find something to stimulate my mind so I've decided to take a degree, then I can work and read beside Jack and so keep him company, but stay alive at the same time. Couldn't face the OU, but the local university is pretty good. I wrote off for the prospectus and I've got an interview in a couple of days. I don't know whether to do Philosophy, English, History or Archaeology – it's exciting! For some reason I was reminded of our Geography mistress at school. She was also in charge of careers. When I left, at sixteen, halfway through my A-levels to look after Mum, who was ill, I recall she took me aside and said, 'You'll be all right Rebecca – in the end.' That was the sum total of my careers advice.

7 September: I went for an interview at the local university today. The prospectus had thrilled me – I didn't realise you could choose from such a fascinating variety of modules – but being on campus was weird. I was the only mature student being interviewed and was hemmed in on all sides by crowds of young people in Doc Martens all clinging to one another skin to skin and shouting 'Fuck!' I say fuck quite a lot myself, but not every other word, and not usually so loudly. It was probably a mixture of collective excitement and anxiety. I felt a bit like that as well. There was an intellectual vibrance about the place, an almost physical sense of expectation. I just thought how incredibly exciting it would be to study. I was such a complete loser at school, I can't think how I'll manage it, but the dear old boy who interviewed me seemed very positive. We'll see.

By 9.30 that evening Jack was already in bed. Will you not come too, he asks, with eyes that have lost their laughter. Oh my lover, not yet. It's only 9.30. But tomorrow night, I promise I will come to bed early tomorrow night.

Graham Brooks invited himself to lunch last week. He's a bishop now, but Jack and he know each other from way back. It was lovely and they were able to reminisce about college days, which Jack could relate to and feel comfortable with, but when Graham talked to me about going to university, and started discussing philosophy (none of which I understood, incidentally) Jack couldn't stand it and stopped me talking. He can't bear me getting animated in discussion now. It makes him feel left out, I understand that, but he doesn't realise how starved I am of conversation. Graham is really urging me to study next year.

10 September: Old friends can't get over the change in Jack. He sits in a cloud of depression. I've come to realise that it was always there – this propensity for *tristesse.* What I didn't know until recently was that he felt this wave of bleakness sweep over him every time he stepped down from the pulpit. When I asked him why, he said it was to keep him humble. He relished public speaking. I'm sure he could stand on a soap box in the middle of Marble Arch and stop the traffic. He once preached at Speakers' Corner in Hyde Park, and was delighted when a woman in the crowd shouted out, 'If you know so much, who washed up after the Last Supper?' But being an orator is very like being an actor; it gives you a buzz to have a group of people listening to every word you speak, especially when you have a melodious voice, as he did, and knew how to handle the pauses. Jack was well aware that he needed to keep his ego in check and he accepted these moments of darkness with the gentle humility that has moved me so much in these last terrible years of his life. He was, he felt, God's son, and his outward ebullience belied the quiet obedience of spirit and trust with which he sat at the Father's feet.

But there is no correlating elation in these depressions now, just a deadening heaviness which is crushing us both.

28 September: I have been offered a place at the university but realise now I can't take it. Can't leave Jack all day, five days a week. I must have been crazy even to think of it. But I feel so angry that he is restricting my life like this. I am screaming inside. Someone has suggested I try Birkbeck, part of London University, because they run part-time evening courses for mature students. I could get a house-sitter for the three evenings a week I'd be away. I've never heard of Birkbeck. It's probably some tin-pot little place in the back of beyond. Still, I'll try.

12 October: The autumn is beautiful. The trees are burning with light. I try to stop and stare, but I don't seem able to relish them. We are in another dip. Jack has had a violent reaction to Prozac. After five weeks of slowly increasing the dose, with high hopes that it would control his anxiety, he awoke mewling with mental anguish and pain. He felt 'suicidal' with one half of his mind. Soon recovered when we stopped the drugs, but we're left at square one. I don't know how either of us will cope with the long dark winter evenings ahead unless we can get help for this depression.

17 October: Had to meet Nicholas at the weekend. We were clearing up one of the open spaces near the park where we're going to hold the street party. We had to scrub the usual misspelt homophobic graffiti off the doors – *Kevin is a homersexual* – but I decided to keep *God is alive and well and working on a less ambitious project*, scrawled, obviously, in a moment of adult despair, though whether brought on by the prejudice of the young or their lack of literacy was not clear.

I'd been anxious about meeting Nicholas again, but it was fun. This time there was a lightness about him. It felt good to be around someone who was happy. He's small but immensely strong, and he worked like a trouper clearing rubbish and making a huge fire of everything we could burn. Before we parted we walked round the park for a bit. I was rather surprised to find that I was chatting away, pointing out things of local interest I thought might amuse him. He loves antiques, and wood, and he began to tell me about making wheel-back chairs, and how to clean old oak.

The silences, when they came, were companionable. Before we parted he turned to face me, and to my amazement, lightly tapped my breast with the flat of his hand, much as you would tentatively tap a small animal you didn't want to frighten. It wasn't intimate in a sexual way at all. It was extraordinary – that strange assumption that he had a right to touch me, coupled with an almost agonising tenderness. I must have looked taken aback. He hesitated, clearly wanting to say something, but struggling.

'I know things are very hard for you … ' he paused, his eyes avoiding mine, focused on my breast, but not seeing, his gaze turned inwards. 'What I haven't told you is that I'm married. I have an autistic son.'

For some reason I was utterly taken aback. He'd always seemed to be a man alone, not in a predatory sort of way. He just never referred to a partner. I had assumed he was divorced, or widowed.

'Josh is severely disabled. He's nearly twenty-two now. He can't talk. He can't do anything for himself. And Helen – my wife – and I, well, it's been a battle really, over the years.' He paused again, struggling into silence.

'Where is Josh now?' I thought it strange that we hadn't seen him, or Helen for that matter, in the street.

'He stays in a care home during the week – he's too big now for Helen to manage when I'm at work, but he comes to us every weekend. Helen and I, most of the time, we live our separate lives. She goes her way, and leaves me to go mine. We're both devoted to Josh. I'm committed to the marriage for his sake, Rebecca. I'll never leave him. I want you to know that.'

I didn't know what to say. I wasn't sure why he'd told me. I was still reeling from his unbidden intimacy. I found myself saying, with unexpected aggression, 'And I love Jack, Nicholas.'

'I know you do, but you have to survive, Rebecca. You have to find a way to live.'

'Finding a way to live doesn't mean letting you flirt with me. And anyway, I am living.'

'No, you're not.'

'What the hell do you know about it?'

'Don't get cross.' He smiled and I noticed his eyes. They were lovely. How come I'd thought him small and brown?

'I'm not cross. I'm just not sophisticated enough for all of this. I don't know what world you come from, Nick, or what you want, but I need to go home.'

I was confused. There was something so incredibly gentle about him, yet he was clearly behaving inappropriately. And there was obviously more to his story than he'd told me.

'If I can help you or Jack in any way, in any practical way, please let me,' he said, and giving me a light peck on the cheek, he turned on his heel and walked slowly away.

I think I wobbled all the way home, and I'm still feeling upset. I can't get the thought of him out of my head. What on earth is happening?

6 November: The weather held for the bonfire party last night. It was great. The church lent us their trestle tables and people came out with huge dishes of food. The kids in the street had made a fantastic guy, helped by various parents, and the firework display went without a hitch. Ryan, who is only twelve but has an actor for a father and a fixation for lighting, rigged up some wonderful lights in the trees, with coloured spotlights on the ground, making the whole area look like a vast stage set. Everyone who had an instrument brought it along and re-lived their youth. The architect up the road got out his guitar and mouth organ and limped through a Bob Dylan. Lisa, who is over sixty, and has recently taken up the tenor sax, gave us a brave rendition of 'Georgia'. James-the-bus (named after his new occupation as bus driver) sang us a couple of musical numbers, the words somewhat obscured by alcoholic slurring, and then the youngsters let rip on drums and acoustic guitars. I sat Jack in a chair along with some other neighbours and he loved it. It was just being in the buzz again that gave him so much pleasure.

Of course Nicholas was there, and to my horror draped his arm around my shoulders as we stood in the shadow of the trees. I moved hastily away. I can't understand this extraordinary attitude he has that he has a right to 'claim' me, as it were. I was uncomfortable.

28 December: Sadly, Dolly, my mother's oldest friend, died just before Christmas. She was in her nineties. She was also my oldest friend because I'd known her since the day I was born. She lectured in Icelandic and Norse at Exeter University and that's where she first met my parents during the war.

Dolly lived in a cob and thatch cottage overlooking the River Exe. It was washed pink on the outside and extremely grubby on the inside since she could never really be bothered with domestics. But the walls were hung with wonderful prints, mostly Gauguin, Cézanne and Matisse, and every conceivable space was crammed with books. I realise now how much of my own taste in art and literature has been formed by Dolly.

As children Michael and I would spend our holidays there, bickering about who would have the bed that looked out over the river. We thought Dolly wonderfully exotic with her blue glass plates and long painted fingernails between which she would crack the fleas that clustered round the ears of her rather disgusting Persian cat.

Her nephew Julian rang and told me of her death, and I went to the funeral leaving Jack at home. I wanted to do this alone. After the ceremony I asked if I could see the cottage just once more.

It had been some years since I'd opened the latch on the gate into the walled garden and walked up to the tiny porch, now laden with overgrown wisteria. The heavy front door swung open onto so many memories. I glanced round the sitting room, conscious that I must take it all in for the last time – the Cézanne hanging slightly askew in its white frame, the long, low bookcases covered in dust, the titles barely discernible after more than half a century of woodsmoke and neglect. The ashes in the huge fireplace hadn't been cleared out. They must have lain there, lifting softly in the draught, for two weeks or more.

The room was just as it always had been, each little knick-knack beautiful, expensive, and grimy, in its appointed place. Dolly's cushions, once so carefully embroidered by my mother, lay squashed in the armchairs, covered faintly in cat hairs, the impression of a heavy body still plainly visible. You would have thought she'd just got up and popped out for a moment, her presence was still so real.

There has never been a time in my life when Dolly has not existed. It was a strange feeling. I wandered into the tiny dining room with its wallpaper of green ivy and the William Morris chairs, and there, on the mantelpiece – also covered in grime – was a picture of me, taken when I was four years old, with long blond hair and a tight little smock, looking very serious. It was the only photo on display and looking at it I felt a deep remorse that I had not kept in touch with her more regularly in her last years, or told her often enough how much she meant to me.

30 December: Nick called round. I thought if I introduced him to Jack that would help me put him in his proper place. Get him into perspective somehow. Normalise things. Jack liked him. Nick offered to mend the garden tap, which was dripping and Jack went with him. He obviously liked having another man around. Nick was very good at including him, so Jack felt he was actually getting involved, rather than just looking on, which he hates. I let them get on with it. Strange feeling to see the two of them side by side. I was very touched by the courteous way Nick treated Jack, with such quiet respect, but when I took him to the front door and said goodbye he gave me the sort of look you hope no one else notices. That's the bit of him I don't trust. Seems cheap somehow.

1995

10 February

Found the first poem I ever wrote to Jack, many Februaries
ago, when it first seemed there might be hope for us. It began:

> The winter jasmine flowers round my door,
> But I have seen them all before,
> These hopeful new beginnings,
> And I'm afraid.

It's nearly spring now. Will he die this year?

3 March: I need help. Have been passing through an extremely
negative and destructive stage, these past four months, unable
to lift Jack out of his depressions and struggling with my own.
People keep saying I will be given the strength to cope. But I
am sick of coping. I don't want to cope any more. I want to
spit out of my mouth all the hours and days and weeks and
years of coping. I've been coping for nearly nine years. Nearly
all of my forties, gone. Now I want to lash out. Part of me
wants us both to die. Yet it's almost frightening how much I
want to survive.

The worst thing is, I have been wanting to push Jack away.
I recoil from him at times. I have withdrawn my affection and

he feels it. I am full of self-pity, triggered by my friendship with Nicholas, I expect, because he just highlights my own needs which cannot be met. But I hate being like this. I want to be loving.

Oh, my lover, how do I maintain the integrity of our relationship? Once, when you touched me, I came alive. Now I scream silently, loudly, keep away, keep away, you are destroying me. Keep away my love, my life, you are killing me. And your heart cries out to me, why am I so distant? Why am I keeping you away? Why can you not stroke me as you have always stroked me, and kiss my mouth? Because I cannot bear it. Because I have no more to give. I cannot bear you near me, you who are all of my life.

7 *March:* How can something so healing and lovely as our marriage turn into something that is as painful and destructive as this? I feel like lashing out at him. Sitting in church last Sunday, the words that kept spinning round my head were: 'I want to die. I want to die.' But I don't want to die. I want to live.

I have to move out of this phase. I have to find a new way.

10 *March:* I have asked to see a local psychologist; I think he is called Martin Dalgleish. Recommended by a friend. It remains to be seen if he can help me. But is help possible? My husband is alive but he is dead. His loving gave me life, but now it is taking my life. And I'm so afraid I'm going to hurt him. I'm so afraid he will see how much this is costing me. I don't want him ever to know how much this is costing. But how do I hide it? We have shared everything. We are like one person. But now I must hide from him, must prevaricate, must act a part. And as I withdraw from him I develop a private life – friends, thoughts, work – none of which I can share with him because he's not up to it.

Mr Dalgleish, help me to be a wife, yet not a wife. Help me to love, but not to love so much. Help me to die to self, but to live again. Help me to consecrate this suffering. Can you do that, Mr Dalgleish?

Saturday, 25 March, 7.30pm: It's a little chilly so I have lit a fire and put on Bach's Flute Concerto. The place looks lovely, a jug of narcissus by the lamp. I love this room. It's civilised, but cosy, homely. Jack sits in silence, looking at the flames. He seems content this evening, but I feel separated off. And drinking too much brandy. We're having a 'holiday weekend', and I'm trying to give him treats to make it seem fun, trying to make up for the distance I've imposed between us. But it's a struggle. I took him to a restaurant yesterday, where they know us, but I just couldn't cope with his inability to talk. Even when I posed a gentle question, an inquiry, he couldn't answer. He just concentrated on eating. He seemed quite content, but I was churning up inside. It took such self-control to just sit there and appear relaxed. The truth is I am full of self-pity. And I know that meeting Nicholas has made this worse. I have to stop that friendship. And now. No half measures, and I have to stop feeling so selfish.

3 April: Had my first meeting with Martin Dalgleish this afternoon. It was unexpectedly comforting. He said I was experiencing both love and hate – I'd never believed that expression before – and that my 'I want to die' episodes could mean simply that I wanted to escape. I'd had enough.

I think what I say out loud, to other people, must be completely different from what I write down here, in private – well, I know it is – because he surprised me by saying I was not in touch with the pain, but looking at it intellectually. I don't think I am, but anyway. He said I was afraid to stop and just feel it. I had to let it overwhelm me – because it won't overwhelm me. He said it wouldn't go away, and if I tried to suppress it, it would come out some other way.

He suggested there could be a way of sharing what I felt with Jack if it was done in a considered way, and not in the raw pain of the moment, which would be hurtful.

It's hard to remember it all with any clarity. I don't quite know what I expect from him. I just know I couldn't bear him to say he won't take me on. We meet again in three weeks and he'll tell me what he thinks. In the meantime, he says, I have to try to get in touch with my feelings. Well, right now I am feeling extremely tearful and depressed.

6 April: Oh, the boredom of these evenings! I've put on some lovely gutty cello music now. It's 6.30 and 'getting dimpsy', as my grandfather would say. I can still see the cherry blossom in the dusk. John next door has burnt an old sofa and with it half of Heather's fence. He's such an inconsiderate sod. Why am I so sad?

7 April: Today I found Jack trying to fill the bath by pointing the shower hose into the wastepaper basket. The wastepaper basket is made of wicker. He was standing by the basin, holding the hose, aqua-planing on two inches of water as it spread all over the floor. How is he able to stand up, he who can barely stand even in shoes on dry ground? I found a way to suggest it might be better to turn the taps on in the bath, without making him feel foolish. I am afraid when I deal with his dementia so coolly. Have I divorced myself from the situation? I put a sheet of glass between him and me and switch to auto-pilot. I just do what needs to be done. I no longer bleed with him. Is this good? Am I finding a coping mechanism? Or is this bad? Does it mean I am not in touch? How would you survive if you stayed 'in touch'? Does it mean I have stopped loving him?

10 April: Jack is more rested today and more in the moment. To my surprise he raised the question of our relationship. We talked, he straining all his resources to concentrate and understand. We talked about the changes between us, about what was worst for him, about what was hard for me, our marriage changing, but still marriage. Just different.

I felt he was not in touch with his feelings, but he thinks he is. MD suggesting it was possible to talk about this I think gave me the courage not to hide, so I was able to say gently that I was also suffering from his illness and had come to the end of my resources. He understood it all, but said he didn't realise I was so low. Why didn't he? I wonder if I hide intense feelings more than I know. He was always so subtle and could pick them up.

Mr Dalgleish had suggested I might be able to share my feelings with Jack when I found a non-hurtful way to do so, and this has happened, surprisingly soon – but do I feel better? No.

This 'withdrawing' that I do, and the changing nature of our relationship, has been happening in patches. I retreat and then rally, fighting back for us both, for our survival. Until the last six months or so I clung on to our old relationship, refusing to let it go, to accept that we were losing it, and I fought against the new. I didn't want this new relationship because, as Martin explained in our first session (I remember now), that was me in a sense 'ending' the marriage while we were both still alive. But I have to try to accept that the marriage as we knew it and built it, has in effect ended and metamorphosed into a different partnership altogether, one that relentlessly increases the space between us so that the love that binds us is stretched to breaking point. I rail against that: I want to fight for all that we had.

But I can't bear these 'good moments' – like flashes into the past – when we can communicate in the old way. It's too painful to go from one extreme to another. And so confusing. Is he really the same, or is he not? Is he demented, or is he not? What is real? These moments of clarity are too painful to bear, a dreadful reminder to us both of what we have lost. And has he lost me? Has this beloved who is losing control of his body, who is losing his mind, his self-confidence, his role – has he lost his wife as well? No. Don't let this happen. I don't want this to happen.

But something is happening, and it's fearful. I am moving away – into silence, into privacy, into an interior life he cannot share. He, who has known by instinct every change of mood, now cannot entirely tell where or who I am. There is something different, some shift, he can't quite put his finger on. I can't tell how concerned he really is, how much of his unvoiced confusion stems from the general deterioration of his mind. I control my voice as I change his clothes, as I wipe the urine from the floor, as I move through life in agonisingly slow motion, trying not to hassle him, trying to camouflage his mistakes, to find tasks and pastimes he can still perform.

There are times, like tonight, when he is still in control, his maturity giving me space, as he always has, his confidence in our relationship intact, sure it will find its equilibrium again, as it always has. But at other times he clings to me as only the drowning can. 'What shall we do now, sweetheart?' he asks again and again and again. 'What shall we do now?' And I want to scream and shout. I feel as if I am disintegrating with the pressure of self-control. I am torn between exhaustion and grief. This is the man who raised his hand high above his head at Kennedy Airport and cried, 'Follow me,' and disappeared down the escalator; arm aloft, quite forgetting that our luggage was still in the belly of the airport bus. He emerged on the up escalator some moments later, his face diffused with laughter but tinged, I was glad to see, with sheepishness.

But I did follow him – into the light and dark of countless human lives. I remember those early years as being full of life. I never knew where I ended, and he began. I couldn't believe two people could laugh together so much. But now he cannot smile, but simply follows me, from kitchen to sitting room, staggering down the garden to the vegetable plot. 'What shall we do now, sweetheart? What shall we do now?' – trying to control the desperation in his voice, anxious not to be a bother, wanting, so much, to help. And my love for him is terrible.

Nick's presence makes things so much worse because he offers what I miss – companionship, conversation – though we don't have enough in common for it to mean much, even if we were both free. Nevertheless I still feel inordinately sad that I must bring our relationship to a close. I feel he wants to find a way to befriend us both, but he's discovered this too late. If he'd realised that before he'd been so tender, it might have been possible. As it is, the wrong feelings have now been aroused in me at least, and the only solution, from my perspective, is to cut them out, bleed for a while, and get on with life. I feel I have quite enough to bleed over, without this!

I hope I can cope with and contain this depression I feel without recourse to drugs. What I would really like would be a four-week break. I'm sure Jack's children would help if they could, but I can't think how, since they all work. I've tried not to let them see how hard all this has become, so they probably have no idea of what's really going on. I'll talk to them.

14 April: Nick phoned for a chat – ostensibly about a show the local drama group are putting on next month. He knows jolly well I'm not interested.

21 April: Jack left yesterday to stay with his children for a long weekend. They live in the same village in Hereford so can share their time with him. He hasn't travelled without me for a long time, so I paid a companion to sit with him on the train – a lovely young man from our church who had just lost his job, so he was glad of the money, and Jack enjoys his company. That saved me the journey and gave me space. This is the first time I have had a moment on my own, without having to worry about him, for months.

At first I loved the peace of the garden. Last night I sat into the dusk just watching and listening. No desire to drink at all. Just had a small nightcap at bedtime. This morning I was up at 6.30 refreshed. I felt peaceful, the stress just fell away. Then I began to think of Jack as he used to be. I was able to capture him again – so hard to do that when he's here. I thought I had forgotten what he was like. But this released real grief. I missed him for the first time and rang him yesterday afternoon. It was the old, real Jack I was missing. Now I feel such pain, but I don't want him to come back. Last night I found myself crying out, 'I don't want to go on, I don't want to go on.' I was shouting at the walls, at the ceiling. I couldn't stop calling out, 'I don't want to go on.'

22 April: Rang Chrissy Lambert and talked for an hour. There's not much I can't tell her. We met in Zimbabwe, though she and her family live in Bristol now. Chrissy is one of the bravest thinkers I've ever known. She has a mind like a machete and a liver of cast iron. She's just started a doctorate in theology – which should ruin many a good dinner party.

23 April: Nicholas called by, just for an hour. I had told him Jack would be away. He tapped on the kitchen door and walked in. He moves so silently I hardly heard him. He drew from the inside of his jacket pocket a single flower. An early clematis. I put it in a glass of water, and as I turned back from the sink he put his arms around me and held me, not tight, but still. I both froze and melted at the same time, but there was more of the freeze than the melt. Then he let me go and we wandered down to the vegetable patch and compared notes on the spring planting.

I was not at peace, and in the end I had to speak. I couldn't just let it go on, with nothing being properly explained.

'Nick, I don't know what's happening.'

'Nothing is happening.'

'Don't be so dishonest. You know that it is, but I don't want this.'

'Want what?' He smiled his irritatingly disarming smile. But after a long moment he talked, not a lot, just in brief, reluctant snatches.

'Josh, our boy, has these terrible, heart-rending rages. He can't speak, you see. When he was at home he used to sit just banging his head against the wall. He didn't sleep, of course. Never, really. Helen and I, we tried, but it was just so overwhelming. We'd only been married eighteen months when Helen got pregnant and we hadn't really settled down together. She'd been very busy then, training as a lawyer. She had to give all that up to look after him.'

'What about you?'

'That was the trouble. I didn't do enough. Not in the first few years. I felt I had to keep earning, to bring as much money in as I could to pay for help and stuff. That's what I told myself. I immersed myself in work. I ran away, really, in the early days, and by the time I realised how tough it was on Helen, how seriously affected Josh was, it was already too late. She was angry with me. She's still angry with me. She felt her life had been stolen from her and that I didn't care. I did care, and I do care, but…'

'So what's it like now, with Josh away? Can't you start again, somehow?'

Nick looked at me for a brief moment. 'Rebecca, she needs me around because I do the jobs. I keep the house and garden going, I pay the mortgage and I help with Josh at the weekends. She knows I'm devoted to him. I also give her space to do her own thing – she's out most evenings at one thing or another, but as far as she's concerned I'm no longer a person. I feel … as if I'm just a performer of functions. I fulfill my purpose,' and turning to me he grew agitated again, his hand quickly touching my face. 'But you're different. You treat me like a person.'

'Nicholas, what are you saying?' The look in his eyes scared me.

'That first time we met, at that committee meeting. There was something about you. When you walked into the room, it was as though someone had switched on the light.'

My God, that's just what they used to say about Mum. I didn't like it.

Standing in the vegetable patch, the sun on our faces, I knew we were in trouble.

'I'm frightened.'

'Don't be. We aren't doing anything wrong.'

'We are.'

'No. We'll just be friends. We both have to find a way to survive. We'll find a way.' And he kissed me lightly on the lips. My own lips didn't move.

I felt both appalled and trapped. Jack was – is – my love. He has been the bedrock of my life. My lover and my soulmate. I have never wanted another. What on earth was happening? And why wasn't I stopping it?

Later this evening Nicholas rang me. He'd obviously been shaken by his own openness. He reassured me again that everything would be kept within boundaries. I felt a little less anxious. But I still worry. I am not sure about him, and I am not sure about me. I find he is in my thoughts much of the time, and I like that. It's as though a tiny spark of life has been re-ignited. He is a light behind the darkness.

So now, Monday morning, I am still alone, and despite Nicholas, or maybe also because of him, the grief for Jack is very near the surface. I am trying to just absorb the pain without feeling I have to do anything about it. I feel I am dying on my feet. No one can help. It just has to be lived through. I am not 'in love' with Nicholas, but there are moments when I dread his departure because he offers me some emotional respite. I know I must end the relationship, but at times I have wondered, doubtless stupidly, if he was in some way a gift from God, since he gives me a level of stability. He alleviates the grief. I feel very sad now, but the words ringing through my mind are, 'All shall be well, and all shall be well, and all manner of things, shall be well.' Those words of Julian of Norwich have so often comforted me these past few weeks. Amazing how a fourteenth century mystic can still speak to us today. She had such an acute sense of Christ's compassion for us in our human state. And his tenderness towards us. I feel that.

24 April: Saw MD for the second time. I told him everything – except about Nicholas – about the grief, about working on autopilot when dealing with Jack's confusions, my fear that I was switching off from Jack and not experiencing his pain enough. But he felt I'd done well. He said that grieving with an illness like Jack's was very complicated and painful, and that the pain would go on, even after his death.

I think what Mr Dalgleish is going to do is to try to get me to accept a different kind of loving for Jack, to believe I have not failed just because it's different. But I feel selfish and negative about myself for wanting to survive, for having possibilities in life, when Jack has none. And I am utterly torn apart by his suffering. I have to move out of this intensity of my loving into another loving, another sort of giving, another devotion, or the pain of this will destroy us both.

27 April: Yesterday I felt again the old longing and love for Jack, as if by getting in touch with it had allowed it to flourish again. It was good, but sad. Jack has decided to spend five days again with his children next month. Although I know this will be good for both of us, and good for the children to feel they are sharing in this part of his journey, I felt real pain at the thought of another separation. The old grief I had been burying is resurfacing. Is this good, or bad? I feel so lonely at the thought of him going.

Maybe I am living on two levels. The submerged level is my totally consuming love for Jack – but it is too painful to dwell in. I did, for many years, sharing with him hour by hour the consequences of his illness. But in the light of the new prognosis, I can't. I have to release myself from such intimacy because it is not bearable. The top level is the 'survival' level, where I live in a less real – or do I mean less intense – world, projecting into the future, a fantasy future, I'm sure. Survival tactics. Knowing this mechanism helps me to cope with it, but I am very near to tears – often quite suddenly – and feel I need to release these, but there is nowhere for me to cry without him noticing, and he must never see the cost of all of this.

1 May: Jack comforted me yesterday, just put his arms round me and held me, but we did not speak. Perhaps we are both afraid to put into words the pain of our situation.

Although there has been a measure of relief in my being more loving, and Jack more himself – though inarticulate – I'm not sure I want to go back to that. It means being in touch with the pain of our situation too vividly. I can't live any longer with that degree of emotional intensity. There are moments, like now, when I feel so utterly desperate. I feel a great strain because Jack sleeps so much of the time and mealtimes are often in silence, yet I cannot leave him because he gets too distressed, and he's unable to go to the lavatory on his own. So I am trapped beside him. We talk very little because he gets so confused, so I feel myself isolated and lonely. And bored. Screamingly bored.

2 May: Had a very touching letter today from Margaret Banda giving me news of the co-operative. It took me back to those wide streets lined with jacarandas and flame trees. And the township, with its cardboard lean-to's tacked on the side of brick shacks, a dusty patch of mealies struggling for growth outside. It always amazed me that despite the unspeakable poverty and dirt, the women would turn out on a Sunday morning immaculately dressed in white. The young boys rolled polythene bags into huge balls held together with rubber bands and played football in the street. Jack could never resist joining in – he'd won a cap in his youth, which now sits on our bedpost – but he always had to win. I kept saying to him, 'For heaven's sake, let the lads have the ball!' But they seemed to like his competitiveness, especially when he cheated and moved the makeshift goalposts.

Looking back, those years in Zimbabwe were among the most fulfilling of our life together – well, for me anyway. I try to remember them, to live them again in retrospect. We learnt a lot, not all of it pleasant, and we made some terrible mistakes. The first, and perhaps the most serious, was the morning Jack patted Betty on the head. Betty was the common-law wife of Aeroplane, the gardener who had been hired by the church to work for us. Jack was a tactile man, but we didn't know then that it was absolutely taboo for a man to touch another woman in any way other than the formal handshake.

Betty, who had spent much of her young life giving herself to anyone who would then feed her, misinterpreted the gesture.

I came home from work that day – I was doing voice-overs for a local production company – to find Jack sitting at his desk in a state of shock. He turned to me as soon as I came in.

'What's up, sweetheart?' I said, since he was clearly upset.

'Betty came into the study while you were out. She plonked herself on my lap and put her tongue down my throat.'

I have to say it sounds quite funny now, but it wasn't at the time. For one thing Betty was a very big girl, and Jack was slight. For another, Jack, for all his sensuality, was an innocent man.

'What have I done,' he said, 'to make her behave like that?'

I immediately went to Betty's little house in the garden and found her sitting on her bed rocking back and forth in a misery of shame and distress.

'Oh, Rebecca, I got everything so wrong. How could I have got it so wrong? I feel so ashamed.'

But I knew it was us who had got it wrong. In our anxiety to be friendly and open, and because of our inexcusable ignorance of social customs (Why had we not done our research properly before we arrived? Did we think we could just swan into another country and take it by storm?), we had seriously transgressed the boundaries of acceptable behaviour and given Betty quite the wrong impression. I felt awful. I sat on the bed with her and held her close. We rocked back and forth together. I knew what it was like to feel shame and it grieved me that between us we had caused her this pain. 'I'm so sorry, Betty. I'm so sorry. It's our fault,' I said. 'Please don't be sad.'

And then we talked. I told her things I hadn't shared with many, if anyone else, and she told me about being abandoned by her stepmother, and how, as a young teenager during the guerrilla war, the only way she could get food and shelter was to sleep with the soldiers. She could never have children because her ovaries were scarred by syphilis. Going to the one cupboard in her room, she opened a drawer and took out a little brown envelope, smeared with mud, that held her medical records. It was all there, painfully clear to read.

The outcome of this misunderstanding was that we grew very close. Betty was in her late twenties, ten years younger than me, she had a big nose and a huge bottom, and an absolutely irrepressible sense of humour. She also had the intelligence and commonsense that, had she been given a better start, in another country, would have taken her a long way, professionally. We'd instinctively liked each other from the first but there had inevitably been a hint of that white woman/black worker barrier. Now, somehow, we were on level ground.

I took her everywhere with me for the next few weeks as I began to research the possibilities for starting the co-operative. Over the next two years she became my adviser and co-worker. We spent hours together making lace, trying to design and produce prototypes of articles we hoped might sell. We went round clothing factories begging for leftover fabrics, we visited shops trying to interest them in our products, and together we gathered the first few women who were to become the founder members of the co-operative they named Kubatsirana which in Shona means 'to help each other'.

And then one day, she left. She wrote me a note.

Dear Rebecca. I am leaving. Aeroplane, he too much talk talk. I'm going to my homelands. I will miss you. Betty.

Betty had wandered off before and returned a few months later, so I was not unduly worried. She knew that Jack and I would finally leave Zimbabwe in the January of the following year, but because of his illness we left two months early. I hoped the bush telegraph would let her know we were on our way. These walkabouts were not untypical among the Shona people. One of our friends, Thelma, had a cook who said he was just off for a quick visit to his family in the bush and he didn't return for thirty years, by which time another cook had been installed. Thelma was so fond of them both she took him back and spent the rest of her life with two cooks. I don't think either of them did much cooking, but it was a very contented little household nevertheless.

Anyway, I thought Betty would come back at some point and I sold my Amstrad and kept the money aside for her – a considerable amount in Zimbabwe in those days. It would have given her a degree of independence for some time. But the day came for us to leave and there was no Betty. To my great sadness I learnt later that she had come to find us the following January as planned, but the house was empty, and we were gone. I never had news of her again, but I have a wonderful photograph of the four of us in the garden in the early days, Betty, Aeroplane, Jack and me. Betty's head is pushed forward like a turtle, caught as she was in the midst of some animated conversation, her gaze fixed on Jack and me, and by the laughter on her face it's clear that she was either ticking us off, or bossing us about. She was brilliant at both. I missed her strength in those last traumatic weeks.

8 May: My lovely Jack, Mr Dalgleish says we are unusually close, not in a bad way, just unusually close. But I told him I was afraid. I am divorcing myself from your illness, cutting you out, putting a glass wall between myself and you so I can see your needs, and meet them, but not feel. Is this good, or bad? Am I finding a way to cope, or opting out?

Have I stopped loving you?

My friend Chrissy wrote to me today. 'Dearest Bex, you hold in your hands the remains of a wife...'

13 May: Nicholas rang and we've agreed to meet briefly. I feel less depressed. I know I have to do something about this relationship. Someone once said, 'If you don't want to go to London, don't get on the train.' True. But I'm on it now, and although it stops now and then, getting off will become more and more difficult. The very thought of saying goodbye to him fills me with despair. He gives me something to live for, some relief from the strain of being the one in control, and a release from silence and loneliness. I fear that if we didn't meet, I wouldn't be able to cope with Jack. Unless I bring laughter and loving into the house, there isn't any. But why don't I feel guilty? Have I matured, or am I burying it? Haven't a clue what to say to Dalgleish next week.

19 May: Jack is with his children for a few days, but apparently very exhausted by the journey. Couldn't speak on the phone when I rang. I feel brutal, as though I've just shoved him off to get him out of the way so I can have a rest. I know he loves being with them, and they need to feel part of the caring, but I am haunted by the struggle to get him on and off the train – those terrifying gaps between the footboard and the platform, his limbs not moving. And having to rush him, thanks to bloody British Rail not coming up with the ordered wheelchair. So there I am, chivvying him along, but his legs won't move and his eyes grow round in confusion and alarm. Feel I'm just adding to his suffering, bundling him off like a bag of old clothes. No matter how carefully I organise things, something always holds us up – a last-minute accident, a mini crisis – nothing seems to run smoothly. There is always some unforeseen eventuality, or a smallness overlooked, that causes him yet more aggravation. I feel such a monster, packing him off for my own self ease. Yet when he's gone I do feel such a release. I feel I have a few days to live again. Should I be deeply grieving that he couldn't speak? I'm not. I'm just shoving it to one side because I can't feel that depth of pain all the time. I have to let it go, just for a day or two.

20 May: A lovely slow, easy Saturday. It's such a relief not having Jack in a chair somewhere. I feel like a different person. Hester came for a chat about a manuscript I've started. It was fun. Nicholas popped round in the afternoon and did a couple of odd jobs round the house. He also bought me a pair of gold sleepers for my ears. Says he wants something of himself to be near me all the time. Why don't I feel guilty? We don't have the same moral base. He thinks if our relationship doesn't threaten our marriages, it's OK. To me, even relatively innocent deception is a betrayal. He thinks that's old fashioned. I think his morality is shallow. The trick would be to avoid meeting altogether! I worry about this all the time. He says stay cool, go slow, wait and see.

22 May: Told MD about Nicholas and how confused I was. He said I doubted my judgment after the intensity of my relationship with Jack. Maybe I would never love again in the same way, but a different way. He made everything seem possible. Nick came round again and we talked about keeping the boundaries, but physically we are always moving closer. I'm not confident he'll draw the line. He's calling by again tomorrow.

I told my old friend Simone about him. She wasn't shocked. She said I was so full of life, I'd still be full of life at eighty. It was a wonderful compliment, but made me realise again why I feel so dreadfully cramped and sad. But she said I must not see him alone, only in company. Wept a lot today – for Jack, for Nicholas, for me. Then Jack rang to say he was fine.

Having a lovely time with his kids. 'You worry too much,' he said. I could have killed him. I could have fucking killed him. I feel utterly tossed about.

23 May: Jack is coming home tomorrow. I don't want him to. I'm angry that he can sound so like his old self. I know he can't help his mood swings, but I feel he is destroying me. This is the first time I felt really aggressive towards him. If he's so happy with his kids, and can talk and join in the fun, why doesn't he go and live with them and not be an albatross round my neck, breaking my back with his dreariness and depression and dependence? Part of me knows this is unfair, but another part of me is screaming out that he is breaking me. And how long will this go on?

I want to write to Nicholas, but don't quite know how. I obviously can't send letters to his home. Anyway, I don't want him to know how much I need him. I'll just write them anyway, perhaps. It eases the loneliness to write. It makes him seem closer. I have this need to keep him in my consciousness all the time. He stops me drowning.

Later on Nick came round. He was mending the handle on the bedroom door, and when he'd finished he held me lightly and kissed my mouth. He's only a few inches taller than me, which is rather a nice fit. But I couldn't make my mouth respond.

'I've forgotten how to kiss, Nicholas.'

'No,' he touched my face, 'It's just that you don't want to yet.' And we went downstairs.

That ominous 'yet'. I am suspicious of his assumption that it's only a matter of time. I am troubled by the strength of my feelings and also the realisation that we might be falling in love. I have been having conversations in my head with him all day. But already I am finding it hard to eat. I know if we have to part I will find it hard to stay alive.

24 May: We have a new neighbour, Maisie. She moved in two doors up and has recently got divorced. She drops by almost every other day with some tale of distress – which frankly I could do without. This morning she'd woken up to find her six year old's hamster swimming for Britain in the downstairs lavatory. She couldn't think how it got there, but had to fish it out and gave it the kiss of life before secretly putting it back in its cage and singing nonchalantly over the Coco Pops as though the morning had started off as normal. Her daughter has enough to cope with, what with her father buggering off.

I'm glad Maisie feels free enough to talk about her problems. It makes me feel less out of touch with normal life. Jack and I are so caught up with what's happening to us, it is so utterly consuming, both in time and emotion, that I sometimes wonder if I'm part of the wider world around us.

The truth is there's a loneliness about suffering that no one can share. It's not that they don't want to, necessarily, it's that they can't. Nor should they. It's not their journey, or their time. Their own grief will come soon enough. It's as well to realise this early on, I think. We can't hold our friendships hostage to our distress. I get upset when our friends want to moan about some everyday occurrence and then get self-conscious in the face of our more dramatic problems. I want them to express their feelings and not always place them in the light of ours. How else can we keep our friendships natural if they are always deferring to us?

25 May: Have been clearing out drawers in the desk and came across some ancient photographs of Dad in those round serial-killer glasses they all wore. There were also some newspaper cuttings in French about his early life. Made me stop and think a bit. About him, about Mum. He really was quite a man, not that she noticed in the end.

Mum never seemed interested in his international work and he blamed her for not supporting him. It was tough being a foreigner in those days when the Foreign Office was a strangulation of old school ties. The fact that he was so much more clever than most of his colleagues, must also have been galling. The support of an attractive woman by his side at the endless cocktail parties and receptions would have helped him bridge the social gaps. But Mum didn't do cocktail parties. She was a countrywoman at heart and a bohemian by nature. She didn't really give a damn about clothes, or fashion, but she could imitate birdsongs so accurately they'd sing back to her. I still recall, as a very tiny girl, standing beneath a hawthorn tree and listening in fascination as she and a robin trilled back and forth, Mum standing absolutely still and the robin cocking his head to one side, his bright eye fixed on hers. Mum's eyes were the colour of speedwells – that extraordinarily bright blue. She knew the names of all the wild flowers and could search out the stars and tell us stories about each constellation.

Even though she was one of the first women to be given a degree from Oxford, what ran most deeply through her veins was not her sophisticated education, but her West Country heritage. There was something darkly Celtic in her nature – that rugged, haunting frailty you find in Gaelic music, the shadowy mix of spirituality and superstition that springs from a landscape of ancient runes and druid rituals. She had a particularly disquieting form of extra sensory perception when she was young. She could hear noises from the past. Dad, who was as prosaic as they come in this respect, told us of the evening they were travelling back across the moor in their little Austin 7 when Mum became rigid with fear.

'Alfred, what's that terrible noise?'

Dad couldn't hear anything, but Mum described the sound of clashing metal, of men and horses screaming. She was absolutely terrified. That evening, back at the university where they were both lecturing, they talked to colleagues and traced their route on a map. They'd travelled through the fields where the Battle of Sedgemoor had been fought in 1685. Fascinated, their friends looked into other reference books and found that people with similar ESP had been documented over the years as also having heard the clamour of the battle.

I know those early days, for them, were idyllic, snugged up in a tiny Devon cottage with their open fire, and the well by the front door. But the war came, and Dad departed, and the long years of separation proved too much for his irrepressible libido. And who knows, maybe there was something about Mum that didn't quite gel.

She should have been a free spirit, but something of her mother's corseted Victorian inhibitions seemed to entrap her in a set of values which were not naturally her own. Was it that? Or was it that the social mores and hardships of post-war Britain tied her to a conventional way of life from which she could see no legitimate escape? It was as if she never quite had the courage to break out of the chrysalis and learn to fly, yet her essential self had the gaiety to fly, and it was this life and brightness in her that so entranced the friends of her youth.

'I loved your mother,' Dad said to me in a unique moment of intimacy, many, many years later. 'I was away for seven years during and after the war, and I wrote to her every day.' But for Mum, love did not equate with infidelity. In the end, they parted.

After he died, and she could be a proper widow and not an abandoned wife, my mother perked up enormously. Her witty repartee returned, laced, sadly, with a spicy vitriol aimed at whatever friend or family member she felt neglected by at the time. I wanted so much to enjoy her, but it was largely impossible.

27 May: Jack has been home a few days, and whatever spark of communication he had with his children has quite gone. He finds it stimulating to be there because he's 'on holiday' and doesn't have to face the reality of not being able to work, and he loves them and can feel like a father again. When he comes home he returns to a cage. He's faced with the emptiness of every day and the reality of his own inabilities, his loss of identity. I do all I can to nourish and entertain him, but there is a limit to what is possible. I feel less frozen with him, but am relating very much on the surface. I feel a part of me has stopped loving him and moved on. I live when I'm away from him – even just shopping. And then there is Nicholas. If I have to send him away, I know I will find it hard to stay alive. I don't mean I'll physically die, but just that it will be hard to be alive. When Jack is himself, I feel guilty. When he is not, I do not. I hope Mr Dalgleish can help me.

But how?

9 June

Dear Chrissy,

What an evening, but I couldn't help seeing the funny side. It involved mother, of course. I picked her up for supper, she sulking viciously because she feels neglected. Mum forgets her hearing aid but decides she'll do her best to engage Jack in lively conversation and does this by placing her snout very close to his – her sight now is practically non-existent – and shouting loudly. Being both unable to see or hear, she has no idea what an intimidating spectacle she makes, especially to one whose brain doesn't function at the best of times.

Jack bleats in weak response, trying to be helpful and courteous, but looking more and more lost and bemused as Mum, unable to hear his answers, develops a dialogue which is completely unrelated to his replies. They finally fall into a stunned exhaustion and wait for me to come and rescue them. I then have to shout loudly for the next fifteen minutes, affecting a vitality I do not have, and dredging from the recesses of my mind titbits of tittle-tattle I hope will amuse them both. Every now and then I flee to the kitchen and clatter the saucepan lids to make it sound as if I'm busy. Inside, of course, I am disintegrating, so I try and think about something soothing – which usually means Nick.

12 June: Mr Dalgleish says I mustn't try to keep him alive. I've got to let him go. How? How do you let someone 'go' who is still alive? I want to fight for every moment of his life to be as full as it can be.

Alison and Toby Williams called. They'd been in Jack's first parish and had stayed close ever since. They were shocked by the change in Jack. Said I was no longer a wife, more of a carer now. No, I am a wife. Can't bear this expression 'carer'. I am constantly referred to as his 'carer'. I am not his carer. I am his wife, his 'helpmeet'. And he is my lover. I will not let him go. I will maximise every ability he still has.

Do you remember when we stood looking across the summer fields splashed with buttercups and knew that we must move on, though we longed to stay? And we tore ourselves away, knowing it was not yet time to rest. And through those dusty, homesick days in Africa we talked each other down Coopers Lane, past the little chapel, past the tile hung cottage, pausing in our mind's eye, for a moment or two, to gaze at the mellow fields where the river ran and where you jumped in with all your clothes on and forgot the car keys were in your pocket. Remember? Rosie's little daughter had got into trouble swimming and you plunged in, with that powerful crawl, and hauled her out onto the bank and then, enjoying the freedom of the water, wallowed about, ducking and diving and rooting among the pebbles for treasure – still fully clothed. We had to ask a couple of strangers to drive us home to get the spare keys, you wringing wet. We got in by borrowing a ladder to break into our own house. Amazing that your watch survived.

Too much moving on and you can never settle again. For me it was enough just to be with you. What was it John Donne wrote about 'our two soules' twinned like compasses? 'Thy soule the fixt foot, makes no show
To move, but doth, if the'other doe.
And though it in the center sit,
Yet when the other far doth rome,
It leans, and hearkens after it
And growes erect, as that comes home.'

Sexy old John Donne. Sexy old you!

Do you remember Eliot who left his wife after twenty years, even though she tried to do what he wanted, including the black silk knickers? And young Mike who died that night, his hand in yours, his parents exhausted, asking you to sit with him. And you did, not seeing the tubes and the bandages, but instead your own dear sons, thousands of miles away, whom each morning you longed to hug, to touch once more. We didn't know then, of course, that your brain was already dying. We just saw the dimming of your wonderful, sparking vitality but never, even in your bleakest moment, did your tenderness diminish.

But now you are dying, though your body lives. And I must somehow let you die, while keeping you alive. I must release the old real Jack and let you go, even as I feed you and wash you and hold you, day by day. As you die, so does our marriage, or rather, as the tangible entity that was Jack changes into something that bears little relationship to him, so our marriage reshapes itself into something quite different. Still loving, still committed – in fact more loving, more committed, because the price of that love for both of us is not joy, but pain. You feel me withdraw, you see me grow more and more exhausted, and you live with the clear knowledge that it is your illness that is the cause. And you are trapped, physically and mentally, and your heart is so burdened. You

> want to set me free, but your need for me is desperate.
>
> How terrible for you, my lover. I hold all the cards, and you have none.
>
> I try so hard not to let you see the price of this loving. I want my love to

be a free gift, but there are stresses I cannot hide. And you, who hate to wait for anything, who don't even want to go to heaven if there's a queue, control your frustrations day by day, and bear your inaction with a costly patience, all for love's sake. How comforting those moments are when we just hold each other and cry. When you are sane enough, and I am strong enough, to confess and share our mutual bewilderment and grief.

But we will also celebrate! Tonight I shall cook you a 'love meal', and light the candles, and make a fuss. I will even make you a pudding. Why not! And we will try to think of some little thing to do in each day, or a person to invite round, that will give you pleasure and a focus to look forward to. We will make the most of what we have, and what we have is a lot. My lover, my love.

An old friend sent me a card which read: *Faith is the bird that sings to the dawn while it is still dark.*

14 June: Ghastly day. J just sits, hour after hour, and I have to be near him in case he wants to get up. He stumbles so much when he walks now and calls out to me if he can't see where

I am. I try to find things to do. Spin a lot, because that keeps me seated, and near him, but I feel quite desperate. Wouldn't survive if Nick weren't somewhere in the background, holding me steady.

16 June: J's presence drags me into such a dark place. I can't lift myself out of it. When he's not in the same room I feel so much better.

Acknowledge everything, however difficult, that's what Dalgleish said. Face everything you feel. Let it overwhelm you, because it won't overwhelm you. Don't try to work out solutions … Life is paradox.

17 June: Another desperate day. Jack dipping in and out of dementia. Why does my perception of what is really happening keep changing?

Annie and Mary, my lovely neighbours, have both expressed concern and say Jack will have to go into care eventually. I say no, never. But they feel I am in trouble.

The truth is, I am exhausted. I want a new life now.

I am thinking of writing to the children and asking if they can keep up the monthly visits until the autumn, and explain that I am going through a crisis and need time to get sorted. I'll think about it.

18 June: Managed to leave the house for half an hour to meet Nick in the park. Felt bad about it.

'Nick, what are we doing? This can't lead anywhere, you know.'

We were sitting on a bench watching a skinny man with calf muscles and black lycra shorts running along the path. It looked such an effort.

'Why not?' He was half-laughing, trying to deflect my seriousness, to coax a smile.

'Because quite apart from my situation, Nicholas, you have a wife, not to mention Josh. Do you ever wonder about leaving her?' He paused then, and became agitated. I had begun to realise that this was always his reaction when he knew he had to speak about something emotional. He'd grown so used, over the years, to keeping his feelings to himself.

'Of course I do. I think about it all the time. I go over all the possibilities. Could I afford to set up on my own and keep the house going for her and Josh? Could I earn enough to support them both? Would my pension run two households? How would it all work during the holidays when he's home all the time?'

'And?'

'I can't see it. Not at the moment. I don't think Helen could cope on her own. Not while he's still at home for weekends and the holidays. He needs us both. Josh comes first. I can't see how it could work. Not yet.'

'So why do we go on meeting, Nick? It's just going to get harder and harder to say goodbye. What's the point?' I felt utter despair. Sensing it, he reached for my hand.

'Because, my lovely, we're making memories.'

'But I don't want to make memories, Nick. That sounds like goodbye. I want to make a future.'

'A day at a time, my love. We don't know what the future holds. Take a day at a time. There's no rush.'

19 June: Feel a quiet, deep despair. Almost suicidal, but undramatically so. The evenings are the worst, I feel so trapped. I really don't want to go on, but that makes me feel so selfish. But heard from Birkbeck that I've got an interview next week. Maybe that'll do the trick. I must pull my finger out.

Saw MD this afternoon. He comforted me by his understanding. He said what I was going through was a kind of torture – Jack dead, and then every now and then a glimmer of him coming to life. He said it was a 'nightmare situation' and understandable that my own emotions were in turmoil, going back and forth. He feels I am still apologising for having needs and see myself as not worth much. Strange, isn't it, that our morality is harshest for ourselves. We view ourselves without pity. How wonderful that Christ is not like that. I feel he is with me, even as I flounder around in this moral maze. He stays close. His love gives us permission to make mistakes. He does not judge. That is exactly what the cross was – or part of it. Christ with us. God gets more and more remote a concept for me, but Christ draws closer in the darkness. There is a little part of me that dares to hope that Nick is something wonderful.

But when I got back from MD and saw Jack so broken, I realised that in daydreaming about Nick, I was just protecting myself from the pain and pity I felt. I have to keep in touch with the grief. It must be faced. I must look the terrors in the eye. That way, I control them. They don't control me. That's the theory, anyway.

And yet I do feel stronger, much of the time. When I first went to Martin Dalgleish I wanted to keep the integrity of my marriage intact. He has helped me to see that, in one sense, that was unrealistic. The marriage, as it was, is dying, but I can keep its integrity by the quality of my care for Jack. This sounds easy to write, but it has been a heart-rending transition.

MD said I feared a 'private' life, because Jack and I had always been so close and I felt that by living and feeling in a way Jack couldn't share, that was a sort of betrayal, but it was not necessarily deceit to withhold knowledge of emotions from another; deciding to make a life of my own was also an act of courage.

I can buy that. But it is a deceit for a wife to fall in love with another.

Yet I do feel now that it's 'all right' for me to be a private, separate person from Jack. It's terribly sad, the result of a tragedy we cannot help, but I no longer feel under the tight constraints I did before. I see that it is sometimes maturity not to share everything.

I find it extraordinary, how Nick has come into my life at just this juncture. Without MD I would not have had the maturity to see Nick for what he is, or to cope with these conflicting emotions. So, progress, I think. MD and Nick coming together has been an answer to my cry for help.

21 June: I had a panic about Nick in the night. It didn't last. I just sat quietly and tried to think things through, and this is how I framed it: something truly terrible has happened to us. My husband, my beloved, is losing his mind. For nearly nine years I have looked after him single-handedly. I have stayed as close to him as it's possible for someone to stay. I have cared for him, carried him, often hour by hour, through his constant depression and bewilderment. I have not distanced myself or spared myself. I have relinquished a great deal of my life – some of which was extremely important to me, like my career – without demur. I have hidden my grief and anger from him. I have given him absolutely everything I had to give, long past the point where there was anything left to give.

Now I can't go on. Other people might have gone on longer, but I am not other people. I want to recognise that I have been faithful. I want to understand that I have to have my own life if I am to continue to care for him with patience and love until he dies – which could be a few years more.

Nicholas has come along at precisely this time. Another woman would resist, but I am not another woman. I need not be ashamed to be the sort of person I am, because the sort of person I am has helped me to love and support Jack in a way which has obviously – even I can see – touched our friends and family. Duality, and lying by omission, will never sit easy with me – God forbid that they should – but I have to have the courage to accept this uneasiness because it will mean my survival, and be to Jack's greater comfort in his last years. I absolutely know that I cannot go on without help.

I feel able to handle the situation with Nick. I don't feel the need to share it with friends – in fact I want them to be protected from it. Nor do I feel the need for the approval of others. Ask MD. Does all this sound like progress – or sophistry?

MD says I must 'bury' Jack and start to grieve. Dear God, am I not already grieving?

26 June: Went to London for my interview at Birkbeck. Now I'm walking on air! There are two great things in its favour. It was originally set up for working adults, so classes are in the evenings, usually three a week. That means I can organise a house sitter, and it's much easier to leave Jack in the evenings. The other amazing thing, for me, is that you don't need A-levels. Instead they take into account your professional life and qualifications, and ask you to write a 500 word essay. I chose to comment on a paragraph by Karl Popper. I had not the faintest clue who Karl Popper was. I had no idea he was a philosopher. Had I known, I might have thought twice, but as I didn't, I just plunged in, strongly contradicting his arguments, and sent off my submission. So I was thrilled last week to be called for interview.

Birkbeck is not glamorous. The main building is old-fashioned and utilitarian. Long cream corridors link one set of rooms to another and there is about the central stairway, with its cream stone and plain walls, the faint air of a public lavatory.

Some lecture rooms reminded me of a Victorian boys' boarding school with inky wooden desks. I would not have been surprised to find bits of old chewing gum stuck to the underside of chairs. Other departments meet in a series of terraced houses in Gordon and Russell Square. These are quite different, their exterior charm complemented by wonderfully haphazard interiors. Mezzanine floors seem to have been added on at whim, stuck in here and there, the narrow stairs and corridors turning unexpected corners so that you have to flatten yourself suddenly against the wall and breathe in to let others go past.

I don't know what I expected at the interview. I was so nervous that my memory has shut down. I remember being ushered into a shabby room with a wooden floor where three lecturers – two male and one female – sat behind a desk. I assumed they were going to quiz me on my critique of Karl Popper, but instead they asked me a little about myself, my work and my circumstances. I told them briefly. I was more interested in what they could tell me.

'So, Rebecca,' asked one, 'what are you interested in studying?' This floored me. There was so much I wanted to know about, and all so disparate – medieval history, modern poetry, philosophy, archaeology – I didn't know quite where to begin. I wanted to tread, educationally, where I hadn't trodden before – which, let's face it, offered a pretty wide field. And I had no idea if I had the capability for any of it.

'I'm sorry I'm not being very coherent,' I stumbled, 'but I haven't really talked about anything much for so long, I've got rusty.'

'If this is you being rusty,' said one kindly, 'then you haven't much to worry about.'

'But how do I decide what to do?'

'Do all of it. Everything connects with everything else, you'd be surprised. Why don't you do English, history and philosophy?'

'Can I?' I said, with a mounting excitement that surprised me. 'All three?'

'Of course. You'd do an Honours degree in Humanities.'

A Humanities degree was new to me. I couldn't believe my luck.

Why had I never heard of Birkbeck before?

27 June: Rowed with Jack. He says will I stop saying 'shit'. Says he's seeing a new side of me, that I'm behaving childishly by losing my temper over little things. I told him it was because I was stressed out and couldn't he understand that? Says yes, he realises that, but even so, could I stop saying 'shit'? I felt so angry. Why doesn't he realise that I have simply too much to do, and am full of grief, and have my own needs not met. He's spent his whole adult life getting other people to do the jobs he couldn't face – like filling in his tax form. And doesn't he know what hell it is for me to be stuck at home doing domestics? Why the hell shouldn't I swear? Shit, shit, shit…

28 June: I love this early summer. Nice little rows of spinach, beets, leeks, French beans and carrots. The broad beans are stocky and the mange tout are snouting happily through. Hope beats eternal in the gardener's breast. This year, we always say, this year will be a fine year for … and then come the aphids and the wire worms. And for some inexplicable reason, the garden these days is hooching with woodlice. Mr Armstrong at the ironmongers gave me detailed instructions on how to erect a screen of old lace curtains to keep away the carrot root fly.

Jack used to look on in incredulity because, he said, you could buy a bag of carrots at the shop for a few pence, so why have all the hassle? Because, I told him, year after year, I can vent my spleen on the vegetable plot when Life, by which I frequently mean Mother, threatens to overwhelm me. Besides which there is a deep, primitive pleasure in working the soil and providing food for your family. You live your life by the seasons, and it gives you a connectedness to the earth and a sense of being grounded. What's more, our veggies are not covered in pesticides. He loves eating the vegetables, let it be said, though I have not yet converted him to the positively orgasmic pleasure of well-rotted manure that has turned into that lovely crumbly, chocolatey brown. I always want to roll in it.

29 June: I was looking at Mum's shock of white hair this afternoon. It's very thick. It reminded me of the picture I have of her as a schoolgirl. Her hair in a single plait. My aunt once told me it was the colour of chestnuts. She's wearing a gymslip in the photo and looks full of mischief. I don't know why, but it made me realise how brave Mum is, when the chips are down.

When I was sixteen she became terribly ill – just because our GP didn't like doing injections and so avoided taking a blood sample. As it turned out, she had advanced pernicious anemia, but we didn't know it then. Michael was at medical school and Dad was somewhere or other. I had spent the New Year holidays in Scotland doing the rounds of the Highland Balls – my one and only foray into posh society – with my sweetheart Sam, who lived in Argyll. I came back on the seventh of January to find a huge snowdrift round the front door and Mum dying gently in her bed. Clara was looking after her.

Clara was the wonderful woman who helped Mum in the house twice a week and kept our domestics afloat. But she was much more than that. She was the rock to which our creative but dysfunctional family clung – and many a time she protected me from my mother's scathing jealousy. 'Nonsense. Rebecca looks lovely,' she'd say, as I appeared in a new dress that my mother, for whatever reason, frowned upon.

I can still see her large, water-red hands, the constant drip from her nose and her powerful body enveloped, as always, in a pinny. She smelt of something clean but not pretty. She was immensely strong, both physically and emotionally, and absolutely loyal. She had attached herself to us and we certainly attached ourselves to her. She would tell us stories about her father who had been a school boilerman and fond of a drink or two. One day he came home and hung his hat on the gas lamp. Nearly burnt the house down, but for some reason the family always thought it funny. We would have been lost without Clara.

This January afternoon I came home to find her ensconced in the house keeping guard over mother till I returned, her trembling husband, with his glass drinking straw and blank face, sitting patiently and kindly in our sitting room. She'd had to bring a camp bed with her so he could sleep downstairs. He had Parkinson's, and in the days when treatment was poor. Dear Clara, I know now a little of what you went through.

In the end the paramedics came and drilled a hole in Mum's breast bone as she lay quietly in bed in her blue crochet bedjacket. I still have it. It's very soft and lacy. Her red cell count, it transpired, was down to 6. They used to give people raw liver sandwiches in the old days, she said. And no, it didn't hurt much. Mum was incredibly courageous.

And so I never went back to school. I was nearly seventeen, and with a relief I can still feel, more than four decades later, I headed, metaphorically, for the hills. In fact I took over the running of the homestead, with Clara's help, until I started training on the newspaper some ten months later.

My brother came home at weekends – sometimes – and would jump over Mum's bed, running the length of the bedroom and hurling a textbook into the air, his exuberance both alarming and delighting her as she struggled to regain her strength. She rationed herself to one chapter a week of *The Lord of the Rings*, which had just been published, and at that rate was about ready to rise again when Gollum slithered to his final demise.

When things were really tough, she never complained, she just got on with it.

3 July: This morning I ask MD what is happening to me? I came to him less than two months ago wanting to stick everything that was disintegrating together. Now, in a few short weeks, I seem to be deliberately, systematically, pulling everything apart. Am I going crazy? Jack is not yet dead, yet I am ruthlessly cutting myself off from him. Emotionally, I feel anaesthetised. I looked at Jack last night and thought 'What the hell am I doing'? It was as if he was as he always has been. Quite normal. He didn't seem demented at all. I feel shell-shocked. Will I wake up screaming someday soon and wonder what is happening? What frightens me most is my ruthless impulse to survive.

MD was so helpful. He said that working out how I was to survive was a bit like being a mother in a concentration camp having to decide which child was to live and which to die. He said it is extremely painful to fight for our own survival in the face of what we 'ought' to do, and in the face of others' expectations – in this case Jack's expectations of me. Such an experience as ours was bound to hurt, but some people came out broken and others with new strengths. All he could do was try to help me have the objectivity to come out stronger. But I feel awful, as though by fighting for my own survival I have turned into a monster.

7 July: Jack's son and daughter called to take him back to Hereford for the weekend. He was thrilled to see them, his eyes bright as he lifted his arms for a hug. They held him very gently, and then we all gathered in the sitting room while they chatted about their work and their children. Jack listened intently, sometimes stammering out a simple question. I sensed them hiding their distress as it dawned on them how disabled he had become.

I made us all lunch, and we behaved as though everything was normal, and that it wasn't a big deal tucking Jack's chair into the table so he could eat, and then half carrying him up the stairs from the basement dining room to the front door. We pretended it was perfectly natural to help a grown man put his arms through the sleeves of his coat and to button it up for him. But when I saw him struggling, with such quiet dignity, up the front path, trying to make light of it all as one foot shuffled in front of the other, I thought, 'Is this really me, cutting him out like this? Is this really me, plotting for my next visit with Nicholas, watching my man, my lovely man, stumbling off into the darkness?' I feel as if I'm pulling the wings off flies.

8 July: It's 10.15pm and dark and I'm sitting on the patio reading by the outside light. The garden is lovely. I have just watered the petunias and geraniums and the air is scented with wetness. The flowers are at full blast. It feels so good to be quiet and free – and cool after a muggy day. For a moment I am out of my cage. I have one more day before Jack returns.

9 July: It has been a glorious, sunny day. Nick took me for a picnic. We lay, propped up on our elbows, at the edge of a field of wheat. Below us in the valley we could see the river winding in a lazy loop through the meadows.

'I feel like a lion stalking you in the long grass,' he said, eyeing me over his shoulder.

'That sounds far too predatory, Nicholas.'

'Well, not stalking then, just watching quietly, from a distance.'

'Waiting to pounce?'

'No, my lovely. You know I'd never pounce, exactly.' And he leaned slowly towards me.

I will never forget that first proper kiss. I'd forgotten how to kiss. At first my lips stayed sort of glued together. Then slowly, slowly, I relaxed. It seemed to last forever, that gentle, undemanding exploration of our mouths, his body pulsing close to mine as we lay on the hard ploughed edges of that summer field, me in my French linen suit that creased like hell. All we did was kiss, and in a way so quietly, but it will remain in my memory as one of the most intimate experiences of my life.

We lay a long time, lazily gazing, tracing one another's faces with our eyes, taking in the wrinkles, the laugh lines, the texture and colour of skin, the sun warm on our backs.

'I can't believe this,' he said at last.

'Believe what?'

'You. Do you know, I can't eat, I can't sleep, and sometimes, when I think of you, I literally go weak at the knees.'

'Don't be so daft. You sound like Julie Andrews!'

'I like Julie Andrews.'

'What! She's ghastly. Those horrendous songs, and that goody-goody voice that makes you want to tear all your clothes off and run down the street screaming shoot me, Shoot me!'

'Sounds fun!'

'Oh shut up, Nick.'

Humming 'Doe a deer...' he unwrapped the picnic – just some bread and olives and ham, and half a bottle of something nice. And six large strawberries. He laid a red napkin on the grass and set it out so carefully, as if it was feast – as indeed it was. We ate in silence, enfolded in a peace I haven't experienced for many years.

What a day. What a gift. It's like when you suddenly rest after a long period of work – it's only when you stop that you feel you couldn't have gone on a moment longer. That's how I feel now. He has opened a window on my darkness. I don't see any future, but I see the possibility of hope, a pathway through today. The secret knowledge of his concern gives me the power to go on loving this broken man of mine, really loving, really caring. Yet as I write and think this I am aware of a terrible pain. Despite all the delight and support Nick gives me, I don't want this. I don't want life to be like this.

10 July

My Dear Nicholas,

This is yet another letter you'll never receive. It's one o'clock in the morning. Jack is asleep and I've nipped out of bed to write. I like to leave the curtains open so I can see across the street to Mr and Mrs Barclays Bank, who live opposite. I don't know their names, only that he works in the bank. He has large white underpants that engulf his belly. He strolls solidly around, unaware that I can see straight through their bedroom window. He has a stomach like Pooh Bear. It's a sad stomach. It's the stomach of a man who looks down mournfully at his empty plate. He can't be more than his early fifties, younger than you, with those small, strong shoulders of yours, but just looking at him I am filled with an inexplicable sense of ennui. It's as if I'm being sucked into the smallnesses of life which appear to have wrapped themselves around his body layer upon layer, turning him into a huge roly-poly pudding. I'm sure he farts gently but regularly under the bedclothes, comforted in a cocoon of familiar odours. I know, I'm being grossly unfair…

The sky is lightening quite quickly now, minute by minute. Maybe others are getting restless too as the day begins to pull them from their darkness. As you have pulled me from mine. I don't know where you came from, or how you arrived on my doorstep. I like the way (now) that you hardly bothered to knock, but just walked in, as if by right. I like the way you don't exaggerate, or offer more than is possible. I like the way you are prepared to wait and let the weeks and years unfold, bringing what they may. I know something of what they will bring – this slow and terrible death that yet will not bring death.

It is now five o'clock and the day has come. Soon James-the-bus will make his unauthorised detour past the shop to pick up his morning papers. His passengers don't seem to mind. None of us can work out how he gets the alcohol out of his blood-stream in time for work. We'd miss his canary yellow socks and his old plus fours. Strange how he brings such sunshine into our lives but lives in such a cloud of misery himself. Misery and Opera. He was Something in the City once.

And now I must move into auto-pilot and love my broken man with all my power.

11 *July:* YES! I'm in. I can't believe it. I can't believe it. Birkbeck have said yes! And the great thing is, because I haven't been to uni before, I'm entitled to a grant. The reading list looks terrifying, but I've ordered half the books already. I want to get started straight away – even though I have to wait till October. Mum was hilarious. Friends came round to tea while she was here. They said to Mum, 'How do you think Rebecca will get on at university then?' and Mum replied,

with casual disdain, 'I don't think she has a chance. Not a chance. She'll never make it.' Good old Mum, ever supportive.

13 July: Jack is more alive than he has been for months. I can't bear it. I need space to mourn and feel angry without him knowing. I can't bear this apparent return to the old Jack, alert and in tune with who I am and what is happening. It's as if he emerges from months of deep sleep and expects to take up life as it was, and for me to be the same old laughing, intimate self. But life is not the same. Our life now is shadowed with unspoken emotions, with hidden griefs, and I have moved on. I have to distance myself from him to survive.

When he's switched off, that's fine. When he returns to some sort of normality, like now, it is devastating. I feel I'm turning into some sort of she-devil, I have such a desperate need to live. I long to be free from these relentless demands.

Yet when the neighbours said again, yesterday, that I couldn't go on, and that I must face the fact that Jack would soon go into a home, I said, 'over my dead body'. I want him to die with the cats on the bed and the smell of garlic in the air. I want to be on the bed, beside him, when he dies.

Nicholas, I did not want to love you. I did not expect to love you, or anticipate the possibility of loving you. I do not want to love you now.

16 July: Trying to live with the new monster me who is free from so many previous inhibitions. I am presented with something terribly destructive, Jack's illness, and positive, Nicholas's love – but working out what is good/bad, permissible/not permissible, feels an impossible burden.

Can a relationship based on lies ever work? I feel confused. When I'm with Nick, I want to belong to him, but when we're apart, I realise I don't. I am horrified at what our friends would say, were they to find out – especially good Christian friends who clearly think I'm so wonderful with Jack. They would be shocked beyond measure.

Nick is going on a business trip to Canada for three weeks in a couple of months, and to my surprise I find, for the first time, that I feel nothing for him. I suppose it is just exhaustion. Today I could easily end the relationship. Yet I can't deny the feelings I've had for him these last few months. But I'm glad he'll be away. I need that time to be with Jack. Everything feels so utterly confusing.

17 July: I must not miss Nicholas in the weeks between our meetings. I must love fully and vigorously, giving myself to Jack and the tasks in hand.

18 July: Drinking too much in the evenings. Trying to diet to be a little less repulsive.

20 July: A few weeks ago my brother Michael asked me what I wanted to do for my fiftieth birthday. I said I'd love a really good French meal – a French French meal. So he and Ruth planned to take Jack and me through the Channel Tunnel – a first for me – to a country restaurant they knew not far from Calais. Yesterday he rang to suggest we tried to find somewhere in England, and for some inexplicable reason I was incredibly, childishly disappointed. It felt like a trauma. Why, for God's sake?

'Don't worry, Bex', said Michael. 'Of course we'll go.'

Why was I so upset?

Dear Nicholas, took Mum out today and she was no more awful than usual – nothing you do for her is ever enough, and I have to tread a minefield through her bitchiness about the rest of the family, I just hate that. The self-control needed to be calm and helpful gave me the most terrible feeling. I felt as if I was going to implode. And the frightening thing is there is no way of getting rid of the tensions inside me, they bring me close to breaking point. I had to tell myself to hang on. It's in moments like this that I feel I can't go on, yet I'm frozen to the spot. I feel immobilised.

24 July: Jack's youngest son Andy is coming for a few days next week, which will be wonderful because it will free me to have some time to visit Nick before he goes to Canada. Martin Dalgleish will also be away. Won't see him for six weeks. That scares me. No support systems. I like Andy. He's the only single one of Jack's children and lived with us for a few months when we first married, before he went to university and moved in to live with his sister. He looks like James Dean! He and his Dad always have fun together, and it will be so good, not just to see Jack happy, but to have Andy's moral support for a bit.

26 July: My last day of being forty-nine! I have a wonderful GP. She has been hugely supportive over Jack. I told her about Nick and that I was thinking of having a proper – or rather improper – relationship with him. I wanted to get my body into good working order – and hide the HRT patches. (Hardly alluring – and who knows what they'd get stuck to?) She sensed my anxiety and ambiguity. She said I was 'a very OK woman', and that the conventions of society were often too stereotyped. 'You have to do what your heart says is right for you and your loved ones. It'll take courage, but go for it, I'll help you all I can.'

I shall never forget that 'OK woman' bit. I respect Dr Scott. Her mother was a flying doctor in Australia and her father a medical missionary. She's got a deep integrity and having her support has given me a huge boost – a sort of permission to go ahead with Nick.

Nick is away at the moment, but I know he's thinking of me, waiting for a week tomorrow, when we'll be together again. This isn't the deep passion I had with Jack, with the whole 'meaning of life' thrown in – but I'm a different person now, with different needs, and Nick seems like a miracle. I told the doctor that. She said, 'People make their own miracles.' I don't feel guilty, but I do feel sad.

My birthday, 27 July, 2.30am: 50! Got up to make a cup of tea and saw my first present – from our little cat Rosie. A huge rat. It was lying on the sitting-room carpet and Rosie was waiting quietly beside it. How she got it through the cat flap I can't imagine. She has never, to my knowledge, caught a rat before. 'You're very clever, Rosie,' I said, and she said, 'I know.' I got my camera, put the rat on a dinner plate and took a picture of it, and of Rosie, who once the button had clicked, got up and slowly walked away. I'm sure she was guarding it until I appeared. What a magnificent way to start a new decade!

10.30pm: What a wonderful day. My sister-in-law Ruth had filled their car with balloons saying 50, and gave me a badge, which I wore proudly on my bosom – to her slight embarrassment! They picked us up at 9.00am and we poured Jack into the back seat where he sat in silence, but clearly pleased and delighted to be doing something new. And off we set for my first ever trip through the Channel Tunnel. My brother had found a wonderful little restaurant a half hour drive from Calais, so the journey could not have been easier – door-to-door chauffeuring, with a happy little bottle of bubbly for those of us in the back seat to drink *en route*.

It always amuses me to drive through France because there is never anyone around. The villages always seem deserted.

Where do the people go? This little place (the name of which I have forgotten) was no exception. The long central boulevard was lined with grey houses, their windows shuttered, and nothing appeared to be moving – not a car, not a cat, not a flicker of litter – nothing – just the blinking of the green cross illuminating the chemist's shop. It was as if all life had been sucked out of it. The main street led to a tree-lined square where the weekly market was held, now empty, of course. We parked beneath a huge lime tree, helped Jack out of the car and crossed the road to the restaurant which looked wholly unexceptional, the glass in its painted brown door hung with the obligatory net curtain.

Never judge a restaurant by its exterior! The food was utterly amazing. It was everything a French meal should be – with surprise *amuses-bouches* thrown in between courses – including a vodka sorbet that was so intoxicating we couldn't manage a second bottle of wine – much to my distress, since we were drinking a lovely Hermitage.

Jack nearly fell down the stairs after going to the loo and the censorious Patron thought he was drunk. We tried to explain in faltering French that he was ill, but failed to impress.

When we got home, and the front door had closed on the day, Jack sat on the sofa and said three words: 'engulfed in silence.' My heart went out to him. That's just how I feel too. His inability to talk traps us both. I asked him if he felt very lonely and isolated. I'm sure he does, but he couldn't communicate it. I just sat as close as I could, my leg draped over his, holding his hand.

5 August: Jack with his children again this weekend and I had another lovely few hours with Nick strolling round the antique shops. We always go quite far away, where we're not likely to know anyone, and so far I don't think we've been seen together. We try to be discreet. We had just a little loving. Go slow, he says, over the physical bit. 'We have other people to consider.' I just melted into him. He's looking after Josh tomorrow, so we won't meet again. But now I feel terribly low. A care worker is coming from the NHS next week to assess Jack's needs. I can't shake myself out of this depression. Am I breaking down?

7 August: Jack home today. It's awful. I can't cope at all. I can hardly be civil. He wants to cuddle up – I just can't take it. But how do I reject him? If I didn't have to relate emotionally to Jack, I could cope. It's being emotional I can't handle. I desperately want to feel and stay sane, but I feel so near the edge. I'm really afraid I'm going to break.

8 August: I had a weird dream. I must tell MD about it. I was back in the garden of my parents' home when Sam, my teenage love, called, asking if I could take part in a drama tour doing all the electrical work and playing the piano. I don't play the piano. I know nothing about electrics. But I felt I had to say yes, I would, if he went through it all with me.

I was still in the garden, presumably on the day the tour started, waiting for him to come. He was late and arrived with only a few minutes to show me how everything worked. I couldn't do it in the time, I knew that. But he wouldn't listen. When I said I couldn't do it, he told me I promised him I could. 'There was someone else there, as my witness,' I said. 'I told you I couldn't play the piano.' 'No you didn't.'

He didn't want me then. He ran up the road and I was running after him. 'Don't you want me for myself alone?' I called. I was crying. He was pulling away, though clearly torn between going and staying. I was aching to go with him. I wanted to stop him, to make him wait for me.

While all this was going on I was aware of an intense pressure of people crowding in on me, all demanding my attention. It wasn't clear who they all were. Mum was incontinent; Jack was crapping in his pants. There was someone with a knife. A neighbour was interrupting my conversation with Sam all the time, saying 'Someone wants you on the phone. You must come. Someone wants you on the phone.' Me: 'I'll come in a minute. I'll come in a minute.'

Mum turned to me with excrement on her face, her wrinkles showing through. 'This has been the worst day of my life,' she said, as I was saying the same thing, but more quietly. No one was listening to me. Everyone was telling me how much they must have my help. No one was helping me. Felt intolerable pain, intense pressure, rejected by all. Woke up.

10 August: Mary died early this morning, before dawn. I have not been able to cry for her yet. She'd been failing for a few weeks, but because she's always been half dead, what with one thing and another, ever since I've known her, we never expected her ever to be actually dead. I can't take it in. I can't believe I will never see her again, fag in mouth, poring over a cauldron of jam, or wrapping up pieces of cake for us all to take home.

Our care worker came this afternoon. He is deliciously camp. He's called Brian and he tints his moustache. Best not to dwell on the rest of his body hair … He nearly had a fit when he saw Jack going up the stairs in front of me with his bum resting on my shoulders as I sort of pushed and steadied. But he was hugely encouraging. Said what incredible dignity Jack had, and how he rarely went into a home where so much love and respect shone through, despite the difficulties. That comforted me. Maybe my inner stress is not so obvious. He has put together a package of care help for us, which he will supervise. At this stage, health visitors will come to see to some of the more intimate problems. Later we'll get someone to help Jack bath and get comfortable for bed, and someone else will come in on the evenings I'm at Birkbeck to heat up his supper. I liked Brian. He's an affectionate man, but very organised, and he made me feel I was coping well.

But I'm not. I feel I'm disintegrating, torn this way and that. I deeply resent Jack. I'm fighting like a tiger for my own survival. It's terrible. I feel like a caged beast. I am roaring inside. My head only just functions at these moments, and my head says I must find a way to deflect these feelings.

And then, suddenly, for a few moments, a few days maybe, Jack is like his old self. We are able to talk at some depth about what we are feeling. I say talk, but I mean communicate, because he hardly talks. But I am astonished by how much he seems to understand. Maybe his mind is not affected, only his ability to speak? Does this mean that Jack isn't demented at all? If so, what has been happening? These moments make me feel I have been pulling away for nothing. And will it ever end?

He recognises at times like this that my distance is due to stress, and then of course, because we have communicated, I feel the old love and connection with him. But I don't want to feel it. I can't go backwards. I can't bear to love him like that any more. It pulls me apart.

The terrible thing is that I can't bring myself to be destroyed by Jack. That may not be very idealistic, but it's real. I want to escape. Since I can't escape, I must break the bars of this cage myself. I must live a double life. The thread of sanity that runs beneath this chaos is Nicholas. I know it sounds crazy, but I do believe he is God's provision for me. Yet how can he be? God doesn't re-write the Ten Commandments just to suit me.

And yet … I think I will talk to Henry Bradshaw. He is a childhood friend of Jack's and a pillar of the church. He and his wife know us well. They've been here often enough, I think, to get a glimpse of what life is like. I will write to them in some detail before I go, and ask whether there is any way in which my instinct is possible that Nick could somehow be part of God's gift, unorthodox though that would appear to be. I need to not just crash into things, but to have worked these issues out carefully.

14 August am: Mr Dalgleish is almost dishy. I saw him strolling along the high street today in his slightly shiny suit, his hands in his pockets, wearing a pair of shades with a decidedly jaunty air. He looked like a minor Mafioso in a B movie – a glorious contrast to his courteous and controlled professional self.

I have offered to give the oration at Mary's funeral, but how can anyone begin to do justice to her? She looked like a witch, with her long white hair stained yellow with nicotine, and those incredibly murky spectacles. But I can hardly say that. She should have died years ago, she had so much wrong with her, but sheer cussedness kept her going.

Stan, her husband, had been in newspapers, working the night shift, so her internal clock was upside down. She wouldn't rise from her bed until 11.00am and didn't return to it until at least 3.00 the next morning. Every evening, before Jack and I married, I would toil up the hill from the station – often having caught the last train home – and dip into M's kitchen for a chat and a little refreshment. The door was always open.

When Stan was alive he used to sit in the corner of the kitchen in a rocking chair, out of the way, while M, fag in hand, launched into a political tirade, or her theories on reincarnation, leaning her hip against the worktop because it hurt her to sit down. In the rare moments when she stopped opinionating, or when the homemade wine came out and mellowed the atmosphere, Stan would start to sing. He had a fund of old music-hall numbers, some remarkably rude, which he sang in a soft tenor with all the innocence of a choirboy.

M had an album of old photographs going right back to the early days when they were printed on glass. The implication was that her family had once been People of Distinction – an implication one never dared to doubt. I relished every moment with her. We all did. She was frequently irascible, irritating, self-opinionated and always muddy. She was also immensely generous, and utterly irreplaceable.

Jack is going to spend a couple of days with some old friends from Bristol at the end of next month. They're both doctors, so they can look after him well, and he feels safe with them. Nick could come overnight, but as he said, 'I don't want to precipitate anything.' I fluctuate between feeling horrified and marvellous. There is also a chance we could go away for a few days when Jack is next with his children. Can I carry this through? I don't know. I just don't know.

15 August: M's funeral. I gave the oration. It was such a privilege. But my thoughts wandered throughout the service, veering between shocked amazement at what I was doing with my life and a steely determination to continue. What a muddle.

I remember MD said it was OK to be in a muddle.

Life has ragged edges.

8 September: Jack went to spend the day with his cousins, who very sweetly picked him up. He was thrilled because he hadn't seen them for a couple of years. They'd all been very close when they were youngsters. They were clearly distressed to see how ill he was, though I'd warned them on the phone. In his absence I arranged to see Henry Bradshaw and his wife. It was devastating. Absolutely devastating. I told them honestly about Jack and what was happening in my life, and that I had dared to hope that Nick was permissible as he gave me the courage to go on living and, more importantly, to go on giving to and loving Jack.

Nothing could have prepared me for their response. He and his wife slaughtered me. They neither listened nor perceived. They took out a sledge-hammer and battered me. Even though I realised that the force of their blows came more from their own disappointments and personal frustrations than spiritual perceptions, I was stunned by the crudity of their attack. They accused me of being a Nazi, wanting to exterminate someone who had become inconvenient to me, to push the disabled out of sight. And how could I, they asked, who had had the privilege of being married when so many other lovely women never found husbands, dare to think for one moment that I was entitled to any other sort of relationship? Was one husband not enough for me? And what sort of message would it send out if I, just because he was disabled, swanned off with someone else?

I was absolutely shattered. They had known me for fifteen years. Jack and I had privately comforted both of them in their own individual griefs and they knew how much I loved him. How could they talk like that? I could hardly drive home and immediately rang Nick, who became hugely distressed on my behalf. He kept saying, 'I can't believe you're crying for me. That you're feeling all this for me. That you've done this for me. I shouldn't have let you go, Rebecca.'

'I'm a grown woman, Nick, I can make my own decisions. I still think it was right to go, but I'm just shattered. Why have they understood nothing?'

The next day Henry's wife rang and said, 'Maybe you are in touch with a deeper truth.' That's all I remember. I didn't really know what she was saying, or why, but I did have the most wonderful experience as she was talking to me. The sound of her voice started me trembling again – with the shock of their onslaught, I suppose, it had been so vociferous.

As she was talking I was barely listening, but I was suddenly aware of what I can only describe as Christ's presence. It was tangible. I felt as if he was literally putting his arms around me and making a barrier between her voice and my being. He was separating me from her. To the day I die, I will never forget that moment. My instant thought about it was this, not that Christ was condoning my relationship with Nicholas, or forbidding my relationship with Nicholas, but just that he was with me. Simply that. In my circumstances, Christ was with me. There was no judgement, just his presence. He was holding me.

10 September: Still reeling from the crudity of the 'counselling' I was subjected to. Re-read my letter to them and can't believe they hadn't understood any of it. Nicholas said that while we're apart he would think of me at 10.30 each night. I pause too, in what I am doing, and so we connect, somehow. Meanwhile I struggle to work everything out.

Dearest Bex, I don't know where to begin really. I'm glad Henry's wife rang you back, and maybe much of this has to do with the unfathomable depth of God's love, which doesn't always conform to moral patterns or social norms. I do believe those norms are necessary, and we all know we live in an age of pleasure-seeking, selfishness, infidelity, etc. But none of these things are true of your situation which has taken you far beyond the simple answers and formulae of Christianity into what is perhaps an intense, confusing and painful encounter with Christ himself, a bloodied, loving, crucified Christ stripped of all the decent garments we clothe him in – Church, respectability, codes, laws, commandments, etc.

I don't think anyone can tell you what to do because you've been led somewhere that most of us dread visiting, along a dark path without signposts. Just don't be afraid of the dark – there is nowhere in all the universe that you can go outside his love, and if you love him back in tears and confusion and weakness then aren't you sharing something with him, something of the mess and excess of living that he understood so well?

It's never easy. Christ is not just a social ethic or a marriage guidance counsellor – he is paradox, love, complexity, beauty and God in all things. It's easy to find God in the respectable things (or at least, people think it is). If you can find him in the desolate, unworthy places, you're very close to the gospel. Ring any time.

Chrissy

I think Chrissy should be the next Pope, but she says she doesn't fancy the pink slippers…

11 September: Saw MD. Thought I saw a flash of anger cross his face as I recounted the episode with Henry and his wife. 'Seems like they're trying to undo all we were working at,' he said, or words to that effect. As usual he was healing and helpful. He even allowed himself to laugh! He understands so much. I told MD I felt utterly flattened, that I had no feelings, that I wanted out of the relationship with Nick, that I mourned the hope I had had. Actually I don't feel the ground gained with MD has been lost, but I'm very confused.

I've just remembered that Karl Barth – regarded by many as the greatest Protestant theologian of the twentieth century – had a mistress who was a Christian, and a theologian, just like him. What a very comforting thought, all of a sudden!

12 September: I like the word paradox. These are the paradoxes I have to juggle with:

1. Jack is alive but Jack is dead.

That is the central paradox.

2. I love him. He is the core of my life, but our relationship has changed utterly.

Paradox: I am a wife, but not a wife.

3. Nicholas is important to me but I am not free to love him as I still love Jack.

Paradox: I want him and I don't want him.

4. What I am choosing to do in the presence of God may be the thing that offends God.

Paradox: I want to be obedient but choose to be disobedient.

5. I have glimpses of real happiness and moments of profound despair and pain.

Paradox: I am both desolate and hopeful.

6. My pity for Jack is terrible in its intensity, but I must not let it get a grip of me or I will be destroyed, and then he too will suffer.

Paradox: I must care but learn not to care so much.

7. All that has been me is gone: job, vocation, relationship to community, outlet for abilities, husband, companion, lover, security, peace of mind, joy, hope. But a new me is emerging.

Paradox: I am almost lost but am being found.

This then, is my reality. I have to live in the mess, holding both sides in tension, the good and the bad, the 'alive' and the 'dead', the certainties and the uncertainties, the hopeful and the hopeless. I cannot expect, at this stage, to know the answers to anything, or even to see any clear direction. I am like a juggler performing in the dark, trying not to drop any balls, and not knowing when the lights will be turned on again and the act come to an end.

I know that I cannot bear the pain of Jack's situation any longer, unrelieved. To survive and provide him with the buoyant atmosphere he wants, I have to have hopes and horizons beyond him. Because I am me, these horizons have included another person, but that person does not threaten what I have for, and with Jack. On the contrary, he gives me the courage to go on giving.

My decision to give part of myself to Nick, and part to Jack, are conscious decisions. I am aware of what I give away, aware of what I receive in return. There is in this a sense of control over circumstances that would otherwise threaten to overwhelm with their very terribleness and complexity.

16 September: Jack in Bristol. Nick arrived for the night. He'd had to travel back from Cambridge where he'd been helping friends build an extension to their kitchen. He was tired and hot and went straight into the bath. I poured him a glass of wine and took it to him and sat on the loo seat and watched him bathe. I'd never seen him naked. His body was so beautiful, so compact and strong. I wanted to cry for some reason. He ducked under the water and washed his hair, combing it back with his fingers so that it streaked like an otter.

Our lovemaking was not brilliant. We were both self-conscious, the chemistry between us subdued by a certain nervousness, but we sat up in bed afterwards and did the crossword, which was gentle and fun. He sensed my disappointment.

'I knew it would be like this, Rebecca,' he said, putting his arm round me and holding me closer. 'But don't worry, we've got plenty of time to practise and it'll get better and better, I promise.' He's very confident! I nipped downstairs then and poured us both a whisky, which we drank in bed. There is something particularly liberating about drinking whisky in bed.

4 October, written on the train coming home from London: My first lecture at Birkbeck. I thought I'd died and gone to heaven. It was Anthony Grayling starting the Philosophy course. He can sound so arrogant on the radio, in his measured way, but as a lecturer, he keeps you spellbound. Two things amazed me. He was able to explain complex matters very simply, so that even though everything you were hearing was new, a foreign field if you like, you felt, at the time at least, as though you understood. He made it all so accessible. And the other thing that impressed me was that he treated us with such courtesy. And enjoyment – as though he liked being with us. Not for one moment was he condescending or overbearing. Heaven knows how many years he's been teaching Descartes – certainly his jokes were well honed – yet he made you feel that his interest in him was still fresh. He clearly relished imparting ideas. For over an hour I sat on the edge of my chair and I don't think I moved. So this, I thought, is what a lecture is like. I felt as if windows in my mind were being flung open and I wanted to throw myself out of all of them. There is so much exciting stuff out there to learn. I never in all of my life expected to feel so alive. I shall always bless the man for being my first lecturer. A bit like your first lover, I suppose – if it goes well, you live the rest of your life in happy expectation! I can't wait for tomorrow when we have our first English lecture. History on Friday.

Later: Came home from Birkbeck at midnight to find Jack lying on the bathroom floor, his feet covered in excrement. The house sitter had had to leave early so he'd been there for some time, and the shit was encrusted. I had to scrape it off with a knife. 'Don't worry, sweetheart,' he said, when he saw my distress. 'It's quite comfortable here.'

You bastard God. You unutterable bastard. The brutal reality is this. If you could stop this, you aren't. Maybe you can't. All this only makes sense if you too are helpless. I could draw close to a helpless God, but not to an all-powerful, all-knowing God who does absolutely fuck-all while my man lies alone on the floor for an hour covered in his own shit. And when I ask Jack later why he should suffer so much, he looks at me with such gentleness and says, 'Why should I not?' Because I love him, that's why not. And because he has served you so faithfully. And because you promised. You promised to be with us. You promised your peace, your underlying peace, in all circumstances. WHERE IS YOUR PEACE NOW, YOU BASTARD? This devastation is destroying us. Such illness is an outrage to the human heart. Damn you, God. Damn you, damn you, damn you.

18 October: When will it end, this terrible turning and turning he does in his mind, unable to fill a kettle with water, zipping and unzipping his flies in the loo because he can't remember why he's in there and what he has to do. The care worker is coming again to assess what extra help we can now get. Have felt quite panicky. I have clung on to Nick in the darkness and it has brought me much strength and patience. I wrap his tenderness around me like a cloak.

19 October: Jack's children have rung with dates for next month's visit and we've arranged for Jack's cousin to accompany him on the train. Guilt and anxiety again intrude – but just a shadow passing before the sun.

9 November: Three exhausting weeks with Jack dipping in and out of dementia. When I got back from seeing Mr Dalgleish the other day Jack was in a terrible state. He couldn't remember where I'd gone, or if I was coming back. And did he have to cook his meal? And how did he cook his meal? It was only three in the afternoon. All sorts of pots and pans were out and I found him looking for a tea bag in the cutlery drawer.

I have to keep in touch with the grief if I am to be his companion in all of this. And I want to be. I want him to be able to rely on me to be with him. Mr Dalgleish stressed again that I must let it overwhelm me, not bury it, but I feel so distraught. And to hide it I put on this awful sort of Joyce Grenfell 'Now children, let's all be flowers' voice and have to keep re-adjusting my tone so that I say, quite matter-of-factly, 'I think I put the tea bags in the caddy, dear', as though it's the most natural thing in the world for a grown man to scrabble around among the knives and forks to make a cup of tea.

10 November: God, you have wounded my love. You have been unfaithful to me. You taught me to think like a child, to respond like a child. 'Call me Daddy,' you said. Why then this terrible and unexpected initiation into manhood? Should we have known, from the cross, that for those of us who follow Christ, there is always a moment when darkness comes unannounced and we are abandoned?

11 November: His cousin came to take him to the children this morning and I have a free weekend, but I feel nervously exhausted. Nick and I haven't met for several weeks, but even so, I'm not sure I'm up to it.

13 November: In the end it was a wonderful weekend. Nick and I drove to Charleston, the house in East Sussex where the Bloomsbury set lived and made lampshades out of pottery colanders and painted murals on everything – walls, doors, tables, chairs. We loved it. We then meandered back home through wonderful countryside, arriving at dusk, and had supper and breakfast the following day, in bed. At one point, when we were talking, Nick said, 'You don't make love to a body, you make love to a person.' I'm not sure how many men know that.

We then spent a glorious Sunday walking along the beach at Camber Sands. It was deserted, and I stripped to the waist, paddling in the shallows and letting the wind blow through my body and mind. Believe it or not, I felt joyful. I felt free and alive. There was one magical moment when a huge flock of Canada geese that had been grazing in the fields nearby suddenly took off and flew in a magnificent storm of wings literally feet above our heads. We felt strangely privileged to have been with them.

Nick knows that had Jack not been ill, all this would never have happened. He also knows that he cannot experience the pain, but he tries to hold it together with me, to incorporate it honestly into our relationship.

14 November: Jack returned from another visit to his children – the last trip he'll make this way, I suspect. His cousin helped him off the train and I was there to meet him. I ran down the platform, waving extravagantly – because it delights him – and gathered him, so dishevelled and broken-looking, into my arms. We got a taxi to Charing Cross. I heaved him in OK, but he had to get out by sitting on the floor and crawling towards the door.

I tried to talk to him all the way home – but he was unable to reply, though he listened. As soon as we got in he went to the loo, sat down, and peed through his clothes. I took off his shoes, removed his clothing, dressed him in clean clothes, making light of it all, and touching him, loving him, but inside I howled and howled. As I bent down to tie his laces, as I stretched round his neck to lay his collar down, inside I was howling like a wolf. The noise inside me was so great I wonder it didn't break out and shatter the windows. I expected the walls to disintegrate. Then he kept saying 'Talk to me then. Talk to me.' And I had nothing to say. Nothing that he would understand, nothing to amuse him.

I don't know why, but I find it so hard, these first few hours after a break, to take up the reins again. Before I left the house to meet his train I found myself lying on the sofa shouting at the ceiling, 'No. No. No. No.' I didn't know how to lift myself up to reach the front door.

17 November: Backward step. Death wishes have returned. Every positive feeling is swiftly followed by a negative one. Am distraught. It's as though Jack has been asleep for eighteen months and suddenly woken up, emotionally.

He sees our relationship isn't as it was, but doesn't know why, whereas I have lived with my eyes open throughout those eighteen months, have lived through the pain of that change, and I can't go back. It's a terrible situation. Jack wonders why we are not more intimate, but it is not bearable for me. I feel bad about putting my own survival first, but I'm puzzled why I feel so determined about it, so cool. Is it that I have deadened my heart, or hardened my heart?

Last night I had to grip the bedhead to stop myself running away. I didn't know how to lie there. The strength of my desire to escape shook me. How do I help Jack to let me go? How do I let Jack go?

The Methodist theologian Neville Ward talks about relating our experiences to what we believe about life as a whole. I believe it should be a joyful giving, but I am not 'giving' any more. Is this because I have given Jack all there is to give? Is this why I can build a largely secret life for myself and live with duality and fabrication with an amazing degree of equanimity?

The truth is, I now feel my life is mine to give or not to give. I am not owned, and I have to withdraw part of it from Jack in order to survive. I have never felt life was 'mine' before, it was always beholden to someone else, or to some set of standards or rules over which I had no control or say.

I know a little of what William Blake meant when he talked about 'mind-forged manacles' – those imposed social values, those concepts of right and wrong, those moral obligations and formulaic loyalties we suck in with our mother's milk and which are a ball and chain to our intuitive understanding of the world and our place in it, so that we have little freedom to discover who we really are, what being alive really means. Sad that it takes such courage to cut yourself free.

Going to lectures is such a refreshment. They restore my equilibrium, and I remember Nick's steady voice telling me I'll cope.

I've been trying to work out what I really think about God. I suppose the root of my spiritual pain is that I feel let down. We were brought up to believe in intercessory prayer, that God would 'intervene' if it was his will. I now know that God does not intervene in human affairs. Either that, or he won't. There cannot be anything more devastating to a marriage than for one partner to – very, very slowly – lose all their physical and mental faculties. It will be ten years next month since Jack became ill. When I see him shuffling across the room, his trousers and pants around his ankles, saying in his gentle, dignified voice 'Are you there, sweetheart?' – those are the moments when, if God were to appear, I would spit in his face.

12 December: Dreadful night, ended up sobbing. Couldn't waken J. I had no sleep because he kept kicking me and calling out. Chaos. Today we managed to talk about it – in two stages – about how we were feeling. It's one of his clearer days, and apart from the difficulty of getting out words, you wouldn't believe he had dementia. I told him of my grief at his suffering and our loss of intimacy, how I hated our separate lives, how I just wanted life to end, his life and mine. The conversation stemmed from me suggesting we needed separate beds if I was to get any rest, but somehow this seems a devastating decision. He expressed − I think, a little hard to tell − a feeling of coldness between us because I was so strained. He found me unloving − what he means by that, I suspect, is that we don't make love any more. I don't think he realises that he couldn't. But as we talked, and shared as best as we were able, the old closeness returned. There is something about our love which is indestructible. He said he had never been so far from God, and I had a glimpse of the quality of our life before − God centred, secure in our faith and our loving. So different from the anguished relationship we live through now.

I realised I should have told him more, so I explained about what MD was helping me to do − to let him go. Jack knows that, at bottom, he is the bedrock of my life. He knows how much I have always, always loved him. It healed the rift between us. But this morning, while we sat at the kitchen table doing our Christmas cards, he could not separate the airmail cards from the local cards, let alone write an address. His mind had gone again.

All day he was sadly confused and sat with his mouth open, eyes closed, listing to one side. I tried to stay close to him, to touch him, to talk to him, to minimise the gap between his reality and mine, but in the end I went upstairs and wept, crying out inside, 'Keep away from me. I wish you would keep away from me.' If he had come up the stairs I would have said it to his face. How awful that would have been.

I remembered later the last sermon he preached in Africa, the last one when he was still able to function, more or less. The text was frighteningly prophetic, 'That I may know Christ, the power of his resurrection, and the fellowship of his sufferings…'

MD feels that the dynamic between Jack and me could be particularly difficult just now − a continuing grief for me to try to let Jack go and find 'life' elsewhere, independently, because he had been my life, the source of life. It's so comforting that someone can see through the muddle to the truths behind it all.

1996

Dear Nick,

What a 24 hours. Got back yesterday to news of a terrible murder up the road. Estranged husband stabs his wife to death, stabs all three children, eight, six and two. The eight year old dies and the WPC who found them and carried the little ones to hospital was not only covered in blood, but deeply traumatised.

I am sitting at my desk overlooking the street. It's six o'clock. I love these couple of hours. I'm working on Joyce's Ulysses. *We had to read a passage before our last lecture and I was so perplexed it made me angry. I thought, this is the most appalling intellectual wankery. Then this lecturer we have – who looks as if he's ravaged by some consuming disease, he's so gaunt – sits on the desk in front of us, swings his legs, and just talks about the book. It was stunning. We were transfixed, and suddenly the magic of this particular passage is revealed to us – it was a bit like lighting a sparkler. There wasn't a flame of coherent comprehension, as it were, just wonderful sparks of light. Mind you I'm struggling to put it all together now, but it's the thought that what was incomprehensible can become comprehensible that so excites me. Birkbeck really is an intoxicating place. Why did I wait so long to get to grips with all this stuff?*

Do you know that we have known each other nearly a year but have spent less than twenty days together, and of those, we often met for only an hour or two?

20 February

Dear Nicholas,

It's only 9.45, but Jack has gone up to bed. I have put out his pills, cleared the commode, extracted the cats from their nest in the duvet – the usual. And I have nearly finished an essay on 'Discourse as Subjectivity'. God knows what that means. Because I'm so used to writing articles I find I can assemble an essay into a reasonably coherent whole without having the faintest idea what any of it is about. If I do get a degree, I fear I shall be just as ignorant at the end of it as I was at the beginning …

I only write these letters to lessen the loneliness of these long evenings … Goodnight, my lovely.

8 April: The doctor realised I was at the end of my tether and Jack has been sent on a two-week break at a lovely local care home. The doc explained to him that I needed space and it would be loving of him to let me go. Dear Jack, he wanted so much to help, so he went willingly, with a husbandly care for my welfare. That was so healing, for both of us.

Now I am at Will and Simone's, just for a few days, looking after their smallholding while they're away. The animals are Simone's province. She has eight sheep, two cows, one horse, countless chickens and three cats.

'Just check the sheep are all right,' she said before she left.

'How will I know if they're not "all right"?' I said

'Well you have to go and look at them,' she said.

'What do sheep look like if they're not "all right"?' I said.

'Well, they look – worried.'

I have just been out in the field trying to ascertain if the sheep look worried. Fizzy, the skinniest cat, was definitely worrying a small, rapidly diminishing yellow finch outside the kitchen door. I walked indoors only to hear cracking noises in the downstairs shower where I discovered Meena, her sister, crunching her way, head first, through a small mouse. This is obviously a busy and industrious household. Or perhaps I was just too late giving them their tea. Bogie, their long-suffering and elderly 'husband' (who tried so hard to do his duty by them when they first arrived, even though he had long been emasculated) has thankfully remained his gentlemanly self and hopefully will do his rabbiting in the dark. He apparently catches them in the night and keeps them in a 'store' under Simone and Will's bed. I shall be sleeping at the other end of the house, I think...

Seeing the chickens was an unexpectedly sentimental journey since one of the little bantams – Cranberry – once lived with us. While we enjoyed a tender relationship – she eating out of my hand and listening attentively to my soliloquies, head on one side, her nearside eye looking curiously into mine – she could not take the overcrowding of a suburban hen run, even though there were only four of them, and had to be moved before she became quite bald with stress. I made the usual cooing noises this evening and she came trotting towards me, pecking and purring, much to the astonishment of the larger, older hens who gathered around and gaped.

As for the cows – sturdy little Dexters with broad, wet noses – we stared dimly at one another across an expanse of dewy meadow. They registered my presence with a sort of moody resignation. The truth is, I find it hard to conceal how very good they taste. Large parts of their brother Albert are at this minute nestling in our deep freeze.

I love sitting out here in the dusk, the daisies luminous in the twilight. Amazing how white flowers bring a garden to life – like light bulbs – at the end of the day.

I first met Will when I was six. We lived in the same village in Dorset, and we've been tangled up in each other's lives ever since. Like quite a few lads in our village he was sent to boarding school, but once the holidays began, Will and his brother John would be in and out of our house with a crowd of other young people. We all grew up together. By the time we were teenagers, most of us played the guitar, but Will had a wonderful singing voice. His rendering of 'Hard-hearted Hannah' became legendary. I wish he'd sing it now.

I always knew when the university holidays had begun because the gate clicked and Will would come walking down the path trailing an assortment of fellow students. I was working on the newspaper by then and it was the nearest I got to University. Mum loved the house to be full. She loved their conversation, and it occurred to me more than once that they probably came to see her just as much as me. In fact there was one occasion when Will's brother, whom I briefly and unsuccessfully snogged, brought his archaeology books round to spend the evening with my mother while I went out with someone else.

It was my good fortune, and of course his own, that Will married Simone, who, not least because of her incapacity to distinguish between man and beast (though she finds man frequently beastly, and beasts never so) has enriched my own life beyond measure. Her painterly eye has opened my own to so many new possibilities, both aesthetic and emotional. And I have to say, she is most fortunate to have married my friend!

So he and I have grown older together like two trees side by side in a field, season by season, with only a few separated years out of all the many we have lived. We don't talk together that much, not intimately. I don't think we ever have. Our relationship has been more one of steady osmosis. And that feels very comfortable to me. It seems I have never existed without him.

24 April: My dear man and I have turned some magical corner. Our relationship is loving and harmonious again. He coped quite well with our time apart. I was surprised. But it's wonderful to have him back home again, though his dementia has returned.

Our lovely case-worker Brian has set up a full care package for us to help us cope, He's organised a male carer to come each morning to help Jack out of bed and to bath him. He came today for the first time. His name is Richard. He has sailor-blue eyes and a permanent tan and manages to combine physical strength with a wonderful tenderness. But Jack was frightened and suspicious of him, and uncharacteristically aggressive.

'Who's this? Who is this man?' I explained and Jack called out, 'No. No. I don't want him. I don't want that.' But I told him I couldn't physically carry him any more, and we both needed help to cope. Richard soon won him round. Now I hear little chuckles coming from the bathroom, and Jack's eyes light up when he sees him, even if he can't speak. He has missed male company.

We also have a home help who comes for a couple of hours twice a week, which gives me the chance to go out for a break or go shopping. These are the only moments of freedom I get in twenty-four hours, apart from the three evenings I go to college. There is very little time to see Nick, only during respite weekends. Sometimes he'll meet me for a coffee, or travel up to London on the train with me, just so we have a few moments together.

Everyone is saying Jack will have to go into permanent care, but I say no. Absolutely no.

5 May: When Jack is as frail as he is today, sitting sideways with his mouth open, looking so demented, I feel I couldn't go on without Nick. I long for the reassurance of his voice and his presence. In four weeks' time we will be together again, and I will see those strong capable hands of his, and feel their touch.

15 May: My beloved was so wobbly and frightened today. Couldn't do anything. I took him upstairs, held his hand as he peed and brushed his teeth. Undressed him. Laid him down, his face screwed up with anxiety, his beard now so soft and white. 'It just goes on and on,' he said. I stroked his hand as he lay there, and read him the Psalms. I begged God to end his pain and take him to himself tonight. He won't, but I hope it won't be long. It could, of course, be years.

I have been clearing out your papers today, my love. Do you remember your sermon on Blind Bartimaeus who stood at the edge of the crowd and cried out? 'Shut up,' they shouted at him. 'Just shut up.' But the stranger in the crowd heard him. Through that vast throng the stranger had eyes only for him, had ears only for him. 'Be whole,' he said, and Bartimaeus, who was blind, who was on the edge of everybody else's every day, suddenly opened his eyes. Bartimaeus could see.

I can't see. I can only see you wandering from room to room, your vest over your shirt, one arm hanging loose, until finding me you whisper, 'What's wrong, sweetheart? Something is wrong.' And I hear you every night whimpering in your sleep, calling out to some half-remembered fear, your arms are lifted high, flailing, and you cry out as if you are losing me, calling me back.

25 May

Dearest Bex,

I don't think there's any way of pretending to understand why all this anguish should be part of the unfolding of God's story among us. The cross doesn't explain, but it does guarantee that the deepest and darkest moments have been acknowledged and caught up within Christ's own life. Maybe that cry on the cross was our guarantee that there is no solitude or struggle or separation that he hasn't experienced and sanctified. Even at the very bottom of the barrel, we still stand on holy ground, not abandoned, but held in love. He will hold you my friend, even when you can't lift your arms to hold him back. Ring me any time.

Chrissy

You bastard, God.

1 June: The social services have come round and installed a hoist in the bathroom to help Jack bathe, and double hand rails on the stairs. There are clinical white hand rails by the two lavatories – I feel the house is turning into a hospital. It's grim. The district nurse came round to give me lessons in lifting Jack from the chair because my back is going, but I can't do it. I'm too short to make it work, so he and I manage in the way we always have. It's amazing how often we're able to laugh about it all. The muscles in my arms are beginning to tear (so I've been told) because I have to push Jack's chair into the dining table when he sits down. I think I'll see if I can go to the gym and do some exercises to strengthen up. What a BORE.

4 June: Jack is asleep, and I'm sitting now in bed, studying for tomorrow's lecture. Going to Birkbeck is the most exciting thing that's happened in years. I shall miss it in the holidays. People from the church are taking it in turns to house-sit with Jack while I'm at lectures, but he's always up when I get home, wanting to hear all about it. Heaven knows what he takes in, but I think he just likes the energy. He particularly liked tonight's re-enactment of the Battle of Hastings which the young lecturers – who look like my nephews – entertained us with. They're fantastic. They seem to like us oldies and throw themselves into the teaching with great vigour and good humour. When they speak, the past leaps into life.

It's in moments like this that I feel liberated. I don't begrudge my man one ounce of energy, but how wonderful, how freeing, to be alive again. The other thing that keeps me alive is Nick's laugh. I love his laugh – ha, ha, ha – it's a sort of spontaneous delight that rises in his throat and spreads out across his face and into his eyes.

27 June: I feel it's the beginning of the end. I am beyond tired. The doctor came round and rang there and then to get Jack into a local nursing home so I could rest. He didn't want to go, but the doc said he must, to help me. He's an old friend of ours. He never lies to Jack, he doesn't pretend. Sometimes he just comes round to our house and holds Jack close, or sits on the sofa, holding his hand. He's not a tactile man at all, and I find those moments deeply touching. Jack seemed to understand that I needed help, but was confused.

2 July: Jack's eldest son Paul rang and said he didn't want his father going into respite care, couldn't I find some other solution? I rang the doc back in desperation and he said there was no other solution, unless they'd like to drive the two hundred odd miles from Hereford and collect him. Paul is coming down in a couple of weeks to discuss the care package I've set up with our care worker. He doesn't think I'm looking after his father well enough. I don't think the kids have any idea of what really goes on. Perhaps I've protected them too much. I try to strike the balance between not burdening them but letting them share in his care so they can express their need and love for him, but unless they lived with us twenty-four hours a day, they wouldn't really have a clue of what it's like.

4 July: The nursing home has a lovely matron, but Jack is in a room on his own. He'll hate that. I can't bear to think of him lonely all through the day, not really knowing why he's there, not really remembering. I pick him up again on Monday. It's just a weekend.

5 July: Delivered Jack back to the nursing home. Not sure how much he understood. Seemed bewildered, but gentle and willing.

6 July: Matron rang up. Jack crying for me. Desperately confused and unhappy. Thought I had left him there and was never coming back. Thought he had been abandoned. They couldn't bear his distress. Would I come and pick him up again and take him home? He is back now, and appears to have forgotten the anguish. He's eating, and we are watching the cricket together. I feel as if my heart has been shredded. I cannot contain the pain of seeing his suffering. But I am so exhausted. Dear God, let us both die. Please just let us both die.

I felt, after seeing Jack so utterly desolate on Sunday, that I could not ever let him feel like that again, but the doc and Matron said I couldn't help it, or him. That he would continue to get more and more anxious and afraid until his mind passed beyond the stage of comprehending what was happening to him.

Although we still have joyous moments when he seems very much himself, even if he doesn't speak much, ever since he came back he has been unable to conduct any sort of communication with me. And he is confused about the simplest thing, like how to stand up. So in my mind I am regarding this as his last summer at home and trying to do all I can to make it a happy one for him, but whether I will ever have the courage to let him go while he has any vestige of understanding, I don't know. I suppose I'm just hoping that the speed of deterioration continues. He did pass a lot of blood over a few days, and I noticed that in the last couple of weeks he hardly eats anything so maybe there will be a physical release before he gets too mentally bad, but I am not in the business of believing in God's mercy.

9 August: His children are very keen to have Jack to stay with them again, but as there is no way he could manage a train, they have paid for him to fly to Bristol airport where they'll pick him up. I'm very anxious about it in case he gets totally confused and frightened. He seems eager to go, and I've arranged for an air hostess to take care of him. I shall be glad when I hear he's arrived safely. He seems quite bright at the thought of going. I just can't understand this mental coming and going. Sometimes I wonder just how damaged his brain is.

10 August: Sod's law. Put garden fork through boot, just grazed my foot. Was speaking to Michael on the phone and noticed two little red lines moving up my leg from the wound. Michael told me to mark them with a biro and ring back in an hour. Lines had moved up over an inch. Drove straight to Casualty. Poison heading up leg for lymph gland (or something). Spent weekend with Michael and Ruth. Couldn't have coped otherwise. What a brother. What a sister.

I collected Jack from the airport. As he was wheeled towards me his face lit up. He said, 'It's not true, my darling!' A whole sentence. When he feels most intensely he can talk. It's as if it's pulled from deep within him. He clearly hadn't been expecting to see me again. We fell into each other's arms, though he is so frail I have to be careful to hug him gently. Then I whizzed him along in the chair – his old self exhilarated by this display of *joie de vivre*, his new self slightly anxious.

12 August: Wise is the saying, that we must take one day at a time. Jack returned from his kids, so much himself, absolutely Jack, only weakened, screwing his face up as he struggled to get one word out after another in such a soft voice I could barely hear. It's like that all the time now. But I didn't see, what I had begun to see so much these last months, someone struggling with disabilities and almost submerged by them. I saw Jack, the real Jack, struggling with disabilities. I can't quite describe it, but it was heart rending.

I so dreaded picking up the threads again, but to see his dear self – at least in part – has given me the kick up the pants I needed to again give him my best shot. All I have. I feel so bad that my resources seem so strained.

His children are coming here next week to meet the social worker and plan what other support Jack and I could have. I want more than anything to be what he needs.

Spiritually, I think I have sunk without trace. I feel no guilt about Nick. I have come to believe that morality is more complicated perhaps than I saw it, and that my own has largely been framed round the knowledge of my father's promiscuity. It has coloured everything. Nick talks sense – but very much in the world's terms, and those are not my terms, but I can't try to work it all out now. I need to wait for a stronger day.

13 August: Exhausted already. Filled with a terrible lethargy. If all I can do now is lie on the sofa and just get up to feed him and take him to the lavatory, OK, that's what I'll do. Have given up. Can't fight any more. Love him desperately, but can't do any more.

Found this card pushed through my door, from Father Michael. It's a quote from a poem by R.S. Thomas called 'Waiting'.

> Now in the small hours of belief
> the one eloquence to master
> is that of the bowed head, the bent knee,
> waiting, as at the end of a hard winter
> for one flower to open on the mind's tree of thorns.

Don't ask anything of me, Lord. Do not ask me to respond – in joy or contrition, in praise or sorrow. Ask nothing of me. I can only stand beside you in the darkness. You must work with me in silence because I do not want to hear you speak. Just stand beside me here, in the silence.

16 August: I have finally relented and dismantled the double bed. The two singles are only one inch apart, but I hated it. The first night (this is the fourth) I couldn't bring myself to go to bed, and when I did Jack was awake, and I wept and wept. I very rarely cry in front of him, but I couldn't keep it back. He managed to sit up in bed and put his arms round me, just like the old days, and say in that dear voice of his, 'All will be well, sweetheart.' Where does that voice come from? It's as if strong emotion stirs the final embers of his brain and brings him back to life for a moment – the same touch, the same voice, the same comfort and peace he always gave me. I was telling him how much I loved him, and the grief I felt for his suffering and all that it had done for us, and he knew it all, and held it all, and me.

It is wonderful to feel and hear again the man that was, to experience the relationship that was. Although I have grown so much stronger through his illness, I know that I shall always be on my own from now on. He was an extraordinary rock and with him I felt free, but utterly safe.

19 August: On the doctor's advice I have visited a care home. God! Beige wallpaper with sprigs of brown flowers – in every room. Brown carpets with dull red swirls. The sort of parsimonious Christianity that makes you want to scream out. How do they think it honours the God who painted butterfly wings to live in this kind of sanctimonious poverty?

The matron was very white and maidenly, in her fifties, and I found myself saying 'He can't do anything because the whole of his brain is completely buggered,' and then hastily switching to the language of piety. No, he can't go there. Even if he is so batty he doesn't know where he is, he shall not end his days there

22 August: My dear beloved Jack is going downhill so fast. Hallucinating, mumbling so I cannot hear, or when I hear, not understand what he is talking about. Sometimes he doesn't use real words at all, just mumbles sounds, in a very conversational sort of way, so they sound as though they should be part of a very reasonable conversation. He has also forgotten how to swallow his food. He just keeps on chewing. I have to say to him, now swallow, and after a while, he does. I have shut off all feeling, and just work on auto-pilot. I wrote to Nick and told him there would be very few opportunities to meet between now and Christmas. I need to concentrate on Jack without being torn in two.

30 August: Chrissy came. Said the difference between Catholicism and Protestantism had been described thus: Catholicism was symbolic, and that's why Christ remains on the cross, and Protestantism was historic, which was why the evangelicals, especially, had to have Christ risen, and were offended by the crucifix.

Daft really, since the death and resurrection of Christ are both a moment in history and a perpetual state. He is forever crucified, forever risen. He dies with my Jack through every moment of his day, yet his risen presence is what we breathe in and out as we stagger, bruised and blinded, through each of these long summer days.

Nicholas, don't let me leave you. Hold me close. Don't let me slide away into this blank, emotional nothingness. Yet I must and will cut you from my vivid memory during these next few weeks as I give Jack all that I have. Just come and find me when it's all over. You give me life.

A friend telephoned. 'Surrender to the day,' he said. I surrender to the day.

1 September

Dear Nick,

Seeing you again after these four weeks was very special for me, even though it was just a quick cup of coffee. But at least I saw your face and touched your hand. Our last parting took courage because I knew difficult weeks lay ahead – though I had no intimation just how difficult. Yet I was glad you weren't there. It meant I could give all my attention, undistracted, to Jack, and that felt good. You were at the back of my mind, but when I thought of you (which was often) it was with a quietness that was calming.

I just wanted to look at you today. To trace your mouth and eyes – and your wrinkles – with my fingers. Just to linger over you. There is a proper distance that I feel between us at this time. That's as it should be. It will mean that my emotions are not divided, and I want so much to be what Jack needs, and for him to die calmly at home.

There is such a complexity of emotions at the moment. Relief that the end is in sight. Pain and confusion on the days he rallies and I think, maybe this is not the end at all. Unbearable pain when I stop and look at his dear, skinny weak legs, with the huge incontinence pad. When I gaze at his face asleep, eyes sunken. I suppose to anyone else he would look like every other dying old person, but to me he has great beauty. I look at him and I am touched by his beauty.

2 *September:* It's been a tough day because I've become so fraught, partly with having so many strangers in the house; Richard to bath J, the neighbour to sit while I go shopping, the nurses and care workers in and out. Sod's law, Heather, who'd been house-sitting for an hour in case Jack needed to get up while I was out, left just as he wanted to go to the bathroom. She's built like a brick shit-house – a very nice shit-house – and can manage him easily, but I stumbled and he fell. He was really angry with me, 'Can't you do anything properly?' So unlike him, and I know it was only because he felt so helpless and insecure. But I nearly hit him. I don't know how I stopped myself. I have never come so near to swiping anyone and I felt absolutely vicious. That's a sure sign that the next respite can't come soon enough.

But it blew over. We know we love each other. We say so each night.

But this degrading pain God is allowing us to suffer, this collective stress that undermines the very foundations of our loving – that I find unforgivable of God. Yet, as I say it, I realise it has not undermined our loving. We love as we always have, but I feel the reason we are more or less surviving is because human beings are tough and not because God is gracious.

3 September: Last evening Jack and I were sitting on the sofa after supper. His hands were soft and I stroked the back of them. I love the shape of his thumbs. They curl upwards, as if they're double jointed.

From out of nowhere, for no reason I knew of, I said, 'Jack, are you ready to die?'

And he replied, so quietly, 'Yes.'

And I, with more courage than I knew I possessed said, 'I'm ready to let you go.'

He looked surprised for a moment, and then lapsed again into silence. It was then I realised that, all these months, Jack had been staying alive for me.

5 September: I prepared a bedroom for him in the garden room because the downstairs loo and shower is attached and we've now been given a full-time live-in carer to help during the day and allow me to sleep at night. She's called Barbara, is from Lancashire, and she starts on Monday. I've no idea how to treat a live-in carer, so I've made the study into a bedsit and assume she joins us for meals. Does she?

9 September: My God, this is a nightmare! But funny too. Barbara, the carer, arrived and was professionally jolly, settling into the study with her little brown bag and walking shoes for all the world as if she was looking forward to a nice break in the Lake District. The first evening over supper – apropos of nothing – she launched into a graphic description of her menstrual cycle. 'Eeeh,' she said, 'it were terrible. It were like raw liver…' She then told us in detail about her hysterectomy. I couldn't believe my ears. Jack has taken such a dislike to her that he closes his eyes and refuses to talk or eat if she's in the room. She seems very fond of him, and yesterday I discovered them hand in hand on the sofa – Jack with his eyes firmly shut. When he heard me come in he opened them briefly and rolled them in conspiratorial solidarity. Good thing he doesn't realise that for the last couple of nights she has been sleeping in his room to let me rest! She is being replaced on Tuesday by someone else, hopefully with womb and ovaries intact.

Jack has now been fitted with an external catheter that I put on each night. That seems to have put his mind at rest and he now sleeps through, but it leaks and in the morning when I go down to wake him up, he's always lying in a pool of urine. Do you want to do breast stroke, or crawl, I ask. And we smile at each other and give each other strength. The dignity and grace with which he bears all this destroys me.

18 September: Jack proposed to me sixteen years ago today. On Waterloo Bridge. My staff thought he'd never get round to it.

19 September. I can't believe the last ten days. The new carer came to replace Barbara – a bouncy little Kiwi called Ali who was even smaller than me. She was full of fun, with a loud bustling energy and a wiggle in her walk that brought a twinkle to Jack's eye. He loved her, but she was hopelessly inadequate at looking after him. She could lift him even less easily than I and kept asking for my help – not the point at all. After a couple of days she bounced up to me – she has a voice designed to carry from hilltop to hilltop and seems unable to modify it for the kitchen – 'REBECCA,' she cried. 'D'YOU MIND IF I RING MY FELLA?' No, Ali, I said, go ahead. Where does he live? 'AFGHANISTAN.' For the next couple of days she was on the phone most of the time to AFGHANISTAN. It was hopeless. She was sweet, but no good at all, and very expensive. So I rang the agency, yet again, for another replacement.

22 September: With what terrible innocence we start each day. Richard arrived to bath Jack and after ten minutes or so I heard him calling me anxiously. He was kneeling on the floor with Jack in his arms, J's eyes rolling, clearly semi-conscious. I told him not to fret, the fit would pass. And of course it did, quite quickly, but Richard was distressed. Jack looks so vulnerable at these times.

Then, late in the afternoon, a large whale-like woman, about fifty, appeared at our front door and announced that she was Enid, the new live-in carer. There was something very subdued about her and I suspected fairly quickly that she had a drink problem, but I wasn't sure. I introduced her to Jack and settled her into her room, where, having asked me if there was anything she could do – I said not at the moment – she stayed.

I'd learned from Barbara not to encourage the carers to eat with us – and besides which, it was the only time in the day when there was any sense of normal married life for Jack and me, so I took her supper to her room and when she'd finished she went to have a bath. When they put the bath lift in for Jack they had had to drill holes in the bathroom floor to secure it, and this was directly above our sitting room. At about 8.30, Jack and I were sitting on the sofa in a mesmerised silence when suddenly water started pouring through the light fitting in the ceiling. The whale had obviously filled the bath too full, got in, and water had cascaded over the side and through the screw holes in the floor.

I roared upstairs to tell her, and meanwhile Jack must have struggled to his feet. I heard a terrible crash, and rushing down to the sitting room found him lying on his back on the wooden floor. I couldn't control myself, I lay beside him, put my head on his chest and howled. I was completely inconsolable. It was just the final straw. He put his arm round me and spoke a whole sentence. 'Don't cry, sweetheart,' he said, 'All will be well.' His sweet voice. His lovely voice. Real words. A whole sentence. The only sentence now that ever comes to his lips.

Now he is in hospital with a badly broken hip. He's to have a half-hip replacement. The stupid young doctor said to me, 'Don't worry, we'll get him up and walking the day after the operation.' 'No you won't,' I said. 'He can't walk.' I tried to explain Jack's condition. I told him Jack could neither walk, nor communicate properly and was having difficulty eating and swallowing, but he simply wasn't listening. He kept assuring me Jack would be up and about in no time. In desperation I told him that if Jack faded during the operation, he was not to be resuscitated. At this the doctor became hugely indignant, arguing that it was not my decision and Jack would be fine. I told him it was indeed my decision, as next of kin, and would he kindly listen. What an arrogant little prick. Michael is away at present, but I'll ring him in the morning and he'll sort him out. Do you know what I think? I think because I'm so much younger than Jack, and look it, little prats like him think I don't care about him. Well, Jack and I have probably shared more passion and love in one hour than that sad little turd has experienced in his lifetime.

All that was five hours ago. Now it's 1.30am. I found the whale sitting fully dressed on the sofa, her bags packed and ready to go. She was clearly distressed, in a subdued sort of way. She says she'll leave first thing. Jack is comfortable, but disorientated. How we go blind into each day.

I rang his children and told them. They should be with us by midday tomorrow.

23 September: The children had a lovely afternoon with Jack in the hospital. He couldn't speak but his face lit up when he saw them. There was a lot of affectionate banter, which he clearly relished. Every now and then his eyes glinted with laughter, which was wonderful to see. They operated on his hip shortly after his children left. They had to get back for work but will arrange another trip down within the next couple of days. I visited Jack briefly, once he'd come round from the op, but he was mostly asleep. Maybe he will die in the night? The nurses will ring if there is any change.

24 September: I now know that Jack will never return home. I've found a wonderful nursing home to move him into once he leaves hospital. The standard of medical care is so good, very caring, and the bedrooms and communal rooms are elegantly furnished but homely. We don't know how much longer he'll live. Could be ten days, but since he's not eating, it can't be much longer. How will I cope with the empty spaces? This will be a desolation. Still can't believe it – that he won't ever come home again. When I got back from the hospital the first thing I saw were his old grey shoes in the hall. I could just visualise his dear, big feet. I bundled up all his clothes for the Salvation Army before I went to bed. I'm returning nursing equipment tomorrow and have asked them to come immediately to take away the bath hoist.

25 September: This has been the loneliest day. A most terrible day. Everyone was away. The children left, Will and Simone are out and Michael is in Wales for a medical conference. When I got to Jack's bedside I found he was almost delirious, trying to talk in a croaking voice. He was trying so hard to communicate and was obviously in terrible pain because his body was jerking, which must have been hell for his hip. I called the nurse and explained that his Parkinson's symptoms were making everything worse, and could he have more painkillers.

'He hasn't complained,' she said. 'He can't talk,' I said. Well, she told me, the doctor wasn't available until he did his rounds. And anyway, Jack was on the recommended dose.

'I don't give a stuff about the recommended dose. He should not be in pain.'

I was beside myself. I rang Michael, who promised to come home immediately. I sat beside Jack all morning and stroked his chest and it seemed to comfort him. In the afternoon the doctor turned up and gave him more morphine. I got the feeling he hadn't a clue what he was dealing with. I was so angry.

Michael arrived at about six and went and spoke to him. Although Michael is a consultant physician, his speciality is clinical pharmacology, so he was able, in his courteous way no doubt, to suggest a better drug regime for Jack. I have never been more grateful to have a consultant for a brother.

'How is he, Michael?' I asked, once Jack was more relaxed and settled.

'He's hanging on to life, Bex. He's not ready to let go yet.'

'When will he be ready?'

'Can't tell. He'll decide. You'd better get some sleep.'

But I stayed beside Jack until late into the night. The staff nurse was very sweet. She gave me a pillow so I could rest my head beside his. I held his hand, and tried to make him feel I was lying beside him. He knew I was there. Eventually we both fell asleep.

The last day

I sat with you all the next morning while you slept, but after lunch they moved you to a side ward on your own. Simone came back with me and we found you sitting bolt upright in bed, clearly hanging on, trying not to die, your eyes open, unblinking, focusing inwards. As we touched your hands the life flooded back into your body like a blush. It was extraordinary. I knew then you had been waiting for me to return. Simone sat with us for an hour while I sang to you the folk songs I sang in our courtship, the love songs you specially liked and the Psalms. You closed your eyes and you listened.

And then Simone left and I sat that long evening through, singing and talking, reciting what scriptures I could remember about the end of time – no more grieving, or crying or pain. And you listened with your heart, your hand loose in mine, until I rose to go. I put my lips to your ear, 'I love you Jack,' I said, and you grunted. The next time I held you, you were dead, and I laid my head upon your still warm breast, so thin and narrow.

So now my work is done. Maybe that is what it means for God to have a purpose for our lives. Not for every day, so we are haunted by every turning we make, every decision we take, but that the overall momentum should be Godward, the cul-de-sacs, the dead ends, not mattering. Maybe there is one special task for each of us. Maybe it is the task of a lifetime, or merely that of a moment. And what it is, we may never know. But I feel I know. My task was to be your companion for that journey through the tunnel of physical pain and mental ruin. To stay with you until that last, long-awaited gathering up.

And I can see, looking back, that so many experiences in my past – of both joy and pain – came into their own, as if every episode of my previous life had been leading up to that one cataclysmic decade when I was to find the resources to love you and keep you alive. It was both hard and easy, the difficulties made smooth by the depth and totality of the love we bore each other, a love forged for us both out of the precious metals of childhood insecurities and grown-up pain. More important, it was made easy by your unbelievable grace and dignity, the gentleness and courage with which you bore it, and by your husbandly love. (How sweet the word 'husband' is to me.) And yet, you know, even while I remember it all – that day you died, and the months before you died – you did not seem diminished to me. Despite all your disabilities, you seemed as whole and complete as ever. It was as if the illness could not, did not, touch your essential being. You died whole and complete. And what a privilege for me to love you through that time. Where I failed, my darling man, forgive me. I hear your soft voice, and I know that you have, and you did, and you will.

And now I go blind into a new space. Where are the walls? I stretch out my arms before, beside – I cannot touch the walls. Where am I now? How big is this space? How vast the darkness seems. How we step blindfold into each new era of our lives. Like Bartimaeus we stand in a mapless place, crowded by darkness and we cry Lord! Lord! with little hope that he is really real, and if he is, no hope that he will hear us.

Did you enjoy your funeral? What did you think of the flower beds? All those wonderful cobwebs strung so carelessly between the leaves, each beaded with dew. From every stem and bush, it seemed, there was festooned a festival of lace, a celebration, the garden bedecked. How lovely of the spiders to make a festival of the day your body was finally consumed to dust. Free at last, my lover.

And did you like the balloons? I had your initials printed on all of them. *J.W.T. Risen with Christ*'. And when I cut them free, all twenty of them in yellow and gold, they floated so effortlessly into the high blue sky and we all stood on the grass and watched them until they were just tiny black dots. 'Jack is risen with Christ,' I said, and everyone answered 'He is risen indeed,' and we gazed upwards until they finally disappeared into the light.

Now your ashes are in Will and Simone's wood, buried beneath a white cherry tree we bought in your memory. To be honest, you're in the hen run, because that was the best place to put the tree so Simone could see it from her kitchen window. I thought you'd enjoy that.

Two years pass

Night is not night as in a period of time, it is the darkness that threatens to engulf, just below the surface of our daily discourse, just around the corner from the unexpected moment of calm. Jack's suffering haunts me still. Its remembrance is like a dog tugging at my hem, nagging me always to look down, to look back, to look into. Recently I have had the strength to refuse, to deliberately turn away, spurred on by seeing a video of him alive and vital. It filled me with a great lightness of spirit. I wasn't anguished. It seemed right and healthy to see him as he was, fit and so vibrant. I can't remember that, you see. I have almost no memory of Jack as a well man. But I was surprised, after several days of contentment, even fun, to find myself suddenly wanting to quietly and unobtrusively die. The night had risen so swiftly and imperceptibly, it took me by surprise. I found myself thinking, 'My work is done.'

But I struggle with this. I want to be able to give again. Friends say, 'Build yourself up, grow strong again.' Surely I have allowed long enough? It's nearly two years, yet I don't seem even to have begun.

Teach me to be still. Teach me to accept that I am wounded, and not to feel so guilty because I am not doing…

Ten years pass

So now you are a decade dead and I have grown ten seasons in the vegetable patch. The flowerbeds have run wild, victims of the weather, glorious with their flying petals. It's a blustery late summer this year and the wind has whirled around our borders and battered the fences and gathered up the falling leaves in great bounds of energy. And I have stood at the bedroom window and watched, season by season, year by year, watched and waited.

The truth is, you wouldn't know me now, Jack. I'm studying for a PhD. I have a new job. The house is full of books. I am a different person from the woman you married. I do different things, with different people. I fill my days. As for God, he has disappeared into a big black hole.

It was sad about Nicholas, though, and I feel that I failed him. After you died I remember one afternoon we were lying on the bed. Nick looked so coiled up, emotionally. He always struggled to express strong emotion. 'Nothing can separate us now,' he said. And I was silent. I knew that he would never leave the family home while Josh was able to return to it, however infrequently. I also knew that Josh would always come first, and that his needs would be at the core of Nick's life for as long as he lived.

I loved and respected him for that, but in my heart of hearts I knew that I could not take on – even peripherally – another human being who had such overwhelming needs as Josh. I couldn't face it again – not even at one remove. Nick deserved a stronger lover than I. All the time you were alive I never thought about that, because Nick kept his family life tucked away from me, out of consideration, I think. And also because he, too, needed respite from the pain of it. Like me, he needed a space to forget, a space where he could, at least for a moment, be a free spirit once again. And I suppose, in the end, that's what we gave each other. A window in the darkness. A moment of light.

We parted six months later, quietly, gently. We both knew, I think, that we had made our memories. I often want to contact him, to thank him, to tell him I still love him, but I hold back. He saved us both, Jack, and I shall forever hold him close to my heart. And so I think, do you.

As for Mum, she died three years after you, but not before a wonderful change had come about. In her last six months she became very vulnerable and it grieved me to see her. She remained valiantly brave as her body grew more and more frail. Virtually blind, as you know, and very deaf, but still with that courage that always came to the fore when the chips were down. I loved her the best I could and from being always rather spiky and manipulative she mellowed and became truly tender. For the first time, I think, since I was a child, I could love her as a mother, without reservation. It was the most healing experience.

I am so grateful for those last few months.

Epilogue

Fifteen years have passed since Jack died.

I remember earlier this summer looking at the Iceland poppies in my border, with their frail but joyous petals of orange and yellow and red, and it reminded me of a poem translated by Ezra Pound from the Greek. In it the poet asks his love to be for him, to live in him as 'the eternal moods of the bleak wind', rather than the transient 'gaiety of flowers'.

That is how I have felt about God at times, on this long journey from mountain top to desert – this dark night of the soul. As I struggled to find a new spiritual reality after Jack's death, I yearned, not for that bouncy assurance of the past, so emotionally vulnerable and intellectually challenged when the difficult questions became unanswerable, but for something altogether less cocksure.

Those around me told me not to think so much, to trust like a child. But I couldn't. I'd been given a mind, I had to use it. I'd watched Jack suffer, I had to make sense of it, and besides, everything within me rebelled. The more I thought about Jack's grace in suffering, and the more I connected with the suffering of others, the more impressed I was by the courage and beauty of the human race and the more offensive the old Christian theologies of original sin and atonement became. I rebelled against the concept that we'd been 'born sinners'. I rebelled at the thought of a divinity that demanded human sacrifice in order to make us fit for communion, and it was inconceivable to me that a 'God of love' could not only sit back and watch human suffering and not intervene, but that such a God, who was reputed to be perfect, could create such an imperfect world, riven, as it was, by illness and natural disasters. Most of all, I rebelled at the simplistic answers people gave me to justify these beliefs.

So for a long time I thought I had lost all faith. I toyed with the idea that there really was no infinite reality at all, only the terrible and wonderful Here and Now. And yet what was 'this great absence that seemed like a presence', as the poet R.S. Thomas asked?

And when I looked back at the life Jack and I led together, those decisions we made in faith that seemed to be an answer to prayer, those deep, almost physical experiences of the presence of God, how could I invalidate them? I could not. In the same way that the autumn does not invalidate the spring, I could not deny the reality of my youthful faith. Every living entity transmutes, turns into something else while remaining essentially itself, and I suppose that how we experience God matures and changes in the same way.

There is no doubt that while the presence of the suffering Christ became increasingly real to me as our own suffering deepened, my concept of God grew darker and dimmer. So it slowly dawned on me that what I had lost was not my belief in a spiritual reality, but my belief in the theology we had been brought up with.

What I had to face was not that there was no God, but that the concept of God I had previously held, and my understanding of how God interacted with the world and with humankind, had been a distortion. I realised I had to unlearn everything and start all over again. I had to find a new understanding, a new language, a new way of thinking about the divine. But how?

I sat in silence and confusion year after year, the loss of spiritual understanding feeling even more painful than the loss of Jack. In the end I came to see that, once again, God had to come to me, to find me and teach me – not to believe what anyone else believed, but to take me into a space that I could find authentic. Most of all, I wanted it to be a place without concepts, that transcended words.

A place, if you like, of unknowing.

It was to be a long and lonely process of shedding the skin of all the old ways of thinking that I felt, through experience, just had to be wrong. I began by trying to sort things out with my mind, and I came to see that all along I had mistaken incarnation for intervention. The cry on the cross, as Chrissy had said, so many years before, was a sign that God incarnate was with us in the mess, suffering with us, sharing the complexity of human existence, but not changing the course of human history by waving a magic mystical wand and putting things right, or, in some moment of cruel, capricious inconsistency, not putting things right.

The disillusioned cry of 'How can God be loving and allow such suffering?' is based on the presumption that God is in control of what goes on in our world. I began to consider the notion that God was not in control, that God did not know the beginning from the end, that God was as vulnerable as we were and that somehow the human story was still being worked out.

I began to suspect another reality too, that perhaps God was not perfect in the way we had been brought up to believe. As I recalled the grace with which Jack had suffered, and the way we worked together to turn our mutual suffering into something positive, I had a real conviction that it was in working with the incarnate that human beings brought about the perfection of our world. God couldn't do it alone. Our relationship with the divine was one of interdependence and mutual need.

As I read other theologians I learned that many now did not adhere to the interpretations of the past that I felt had kept, not just me, but so many people in chains. While humankind was indeed a complexity of contradictions, it was Richard Rohr in *Things Hidden* who pointed out that as people made in the image of God our core was in fact original blessing, not original sin.

For scholars like Marcus Borg, the significance of the incarnation and the Jesus story was that it showed the dichotomy between the finite and the infinite to be false, the pattern of his thought and life revealing how we can become more fully human by connecting with that of the divine within us. That made perfect sense to me. I had always related to the Hindu understanding of the self or soul within being connected to, a part of, the Self or Soul without. Our earthly journey was about the consummation of the two.

Yet even as my mind is calmed by these new perceptions that have validated my own discomfort over the years, the inner struggle for spiritual connection remains and I know that, for me, that connection has to be made without words, without concepts, without mind. How can we even begin to wrap a thought around that which is Ineffable? To do so would be to reduce God to the smallness of our understandings. We cannot name the unnameable – a truth the Jewish people have always known.

People say we come around, in the end, to a place of simplicity, or rather, a place of spiritual stillness, poised between knowing and unknowing, to a place where no answers are needed, because no questions are asked. We learn to suspend thought, to suspend emotion and to try merely to be in the Presence we seek. Those are rare but wonderful moments, too often, for me, broken by periods of restless questioning when the mind scrabbles away at the surface of understanding, wanting to know why and how and if, to define that which cannot be defined. But I worry less about it all now.

It was Chrissy who first taught me about spiritual paradox, Mr Dalgleish who helped me live with the paradox of self, and the long journey through the spiritual desert that has helped me to be content to live, not in the bright light of certainty, with all its brashness, but in a dimmer light, glimpsing only rarely, out of the corner of my eye, that which cannot be properly expressed. I do not know what I mean by 'God'. I dislike the word because it is hung with connotations I think unhelpful, even harmful, but I live in a growing trust that we are, as Jung would say, related to something infinite. More than that, I believe this relationship can be intimate.

At times I wonder, with Tagore 'by what dim shore … by what far edge of the frowning forest … You are treading Your course to come to me, my Friend?' On good days I am content to wait and see. I try to hear with my mind, and the thought evaporates. I turn towards a moment of light, and it vanishes. But if I don't move, don't try, if I just rest in complete internal silence, then I think sometimes, for the smallest moment, I sense, like blind Bartimaeus, the beloved stranger moving towards me in the crowd of the day. I wait for his touch.

Diffuse Cortical Lewy Body Disease*

Dementia with Lewy bodies (DLB) was only formally recognised as a disease in the late 1990s but has now been established as the second most common senile degenerative dementia after Alzheimer's disease. Jack was thought to be one of the first patients to receive this diagnosis.

Despite its prevalence, DLB is not well known. Many health professionals aren't well informed about it and patients are often wrongly diagnosed as having Parkinson's or Alzheimer's.

The central clinical feature required for a diagnosis of DLB is a progressive and fluctuating cognitive impairment. Periods of being alert and coherent alternate with periods of being confused and unresponsive to questions. The abilities of the affected persons often fluctuate from hour to hour, and over weeks and months. This sometimes causes carers to doubt whether patients are genuinely confused.

Patients also suffer visual hallucinations, systematised delusions and spontaneous Parkinsonian symptoms like slowness of movement, stiffness and tremor. Repeated falls, fainting, transient loss of consciousness and neuroleptic sensitivity are also clinically characteristic. The disease affects their language, their ability to carry out simple actions, to judge distances and their ability to reason. There is no cure for Lewy body disease, and it usually ends in death, often progressing more quickly than Alzheimer's.

(* Taken from an amalgam of sources.)